Scene Painting Projects for Theatre

Scene Painting Projects for Theatre

STEPHEN SHERWIN

First Edition

Focal Press
Taylor & Francis Group

NEW YORK AND LONDON

First published 2006

This edition published 2013
by Focal Press
70 Blanchard Road, Suite 402, Burlington, MA 01803

Simultaneously published in the UK
by Focal Press
2 Park Square, Milton Park, Abingdon, Oxon OX14 4RN

Focal Press is an imprint of the Taylor & Francis Group, an informa business

Notices

Practitioners and researchers must always rely on their own experience and knowledge
in evaluating and using any information, methods, compounds, or experiments described
herein. In using such information or methods they should be mindful of their own safety
and the safety of others, including parties for whom they have a professional responsibility.

To the fullest extent of the law, neither the Publisher nor the authors, contributors, or
editors, assume any liability for any injury and/or damage to persons or property as a matter
of products liability, negligence or otherwise, or from any use or operation of any methods,
products, instructions, or ideas contained in the material herein.

Library of Congress Cataloging-in-Publication Data
Sherwin, Stephen.
  Scene painting projects for theatre / Stephen Sherwin.
    p. cm.
  ISBN-13: 978-0-240-80813-0 (pbk. : alk. paper)
  ISBN-10: 0-240-80813-4 (pbk. : alk. paper)
  1. Theaters—Stage-setting and scenery. 2. Scene painting. I. Title.
  PN2091.S8S513 2007
  792.02′5—dc22

                                                                2006011126

British Library Cataloguing-in-Publication Data
A catalogue record for this book is available from the British Library.

ISBN 13: 978-0-240-80813-0 (hbk)

To Susan

Contents

Paint Elevations

An Overview

Project 1
Texture techniques

Page 1

Project 2
Spattered and sponged wall

Page 13

Project 3
Distressed wall with wainscot

Page 21

Project 4
Wall with beveled block

Page 33

Project 5
Weathered wood

Page 43

Project 6
Stylized landscape

Page 57

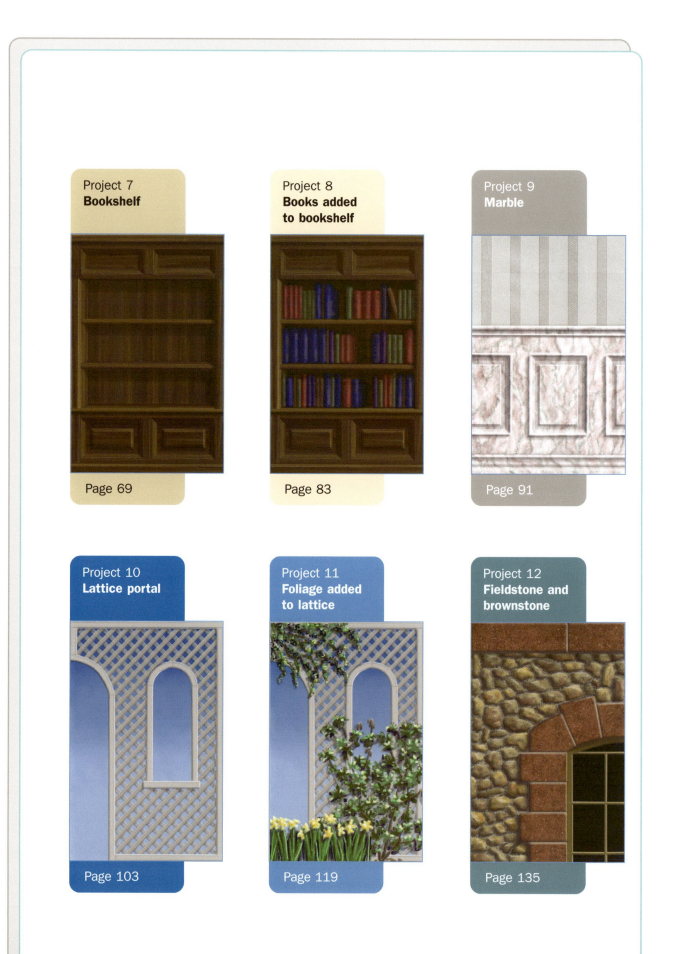

Project 7
Bookshelf

Page 69

Project 8
**Books added
to bookshelf**

Page 83

Project 9
Marble

Page 91

Project 10
Lattice portal

Page 103

Project 11
**Foliage added
to lattice**

Page 119

Project 12
**Fieldstone and
brownstone**

Page 135

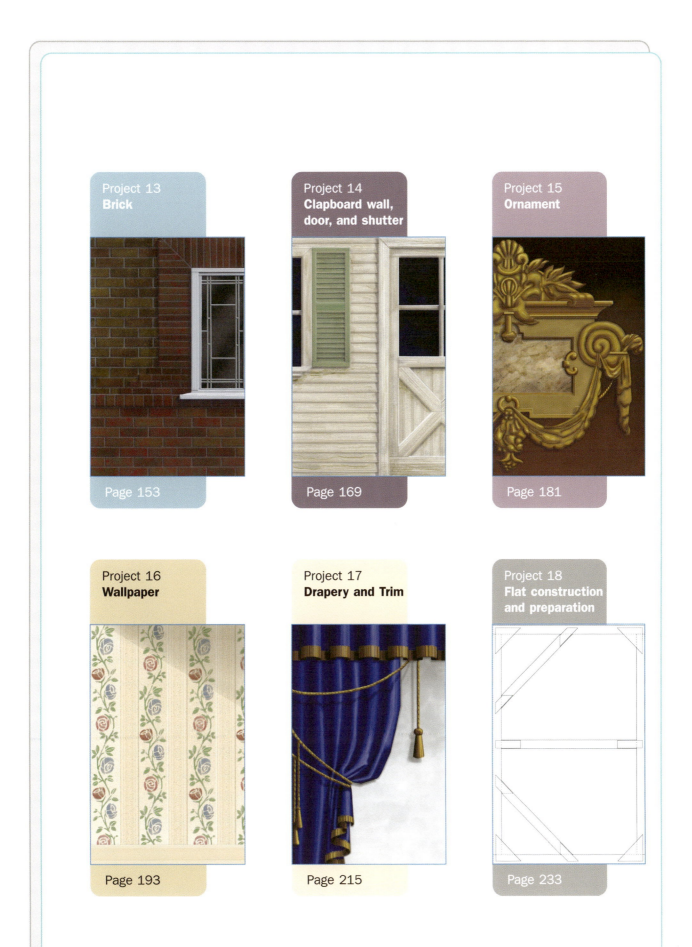

Color Samples

ROSCO Off Broadway	ROSCO Iddings Deep Colors	Sherwin-Williams	Benjamin Moore
Black #5352	Black #5552	Tricorn Black #SW 6258	jet black #2120-10
Yellow Ochre #5353	Yellow Ochre #5553	Gold Coast #SW 6376	spicy mustard #2154-20
Burnt Umber #5354	Burnt Umber #5554	Turkish Coffee #SW 6076	deep taupe #2111-10
Raw Sienna #5355	Raw Sienna #5555	Gallant Gold #SW 6391	golden bark #2153-10
Burnt Sienna #5356	Burnt Sienna #5556	Canyon Clay #SW 6054	pancake syrup #2104-10
Raw Umber #5357	Raw Umber #5557	Sable #SW 6083	otter brown #2137-10
Ultramarine Blue #5359	Ultramarine Blue #5559	Honorable Blue #SW 6811	starry night blue #2067-10
Fire Red #5360	Red #5560	Lusty Red #SW 6863	vermilion #2002-10
Deep Red #5361	Deep Red #5361	Poinsettia #SW 6594	deep rose #2004-10
Emerald Green #5364	Emerald Green #5564	Kilkenny #SW 6740	yellow green #2033-10
Chrome Oxide Green #5365	Chrome Oxide Green #5565	Isle Of Pines #SW 6461	hunter green #2041-10
Lemon Yellow #5366	Lemon Yellow #5566	Forsythia #SW 6907	banana yellow #2022-40
Purple #5368	Purple #5568	Valiant Violet #SW 6818	grape gum #2068-20
Sky Blue #5372	Cerulean Blue #5572	Dynamic Blue #SW 6958	utah sky #2065-40
Pthalo Blue #5373	Navy Blue #5573	Hyper Blue #SW 6258965	brilliant blue #2065-20

NOTES

- *Off Broadway* is one of Rosco's most popular brands of scene paint. It has a matte finish, is water soluble, and has a vinyl acrylic binder.

- *Iddings Deep Colors* is Rosco's high-quality concentrated scene paint. It has a matte finish, is water soluble, and has a casein (organic soy protein) binder.

- *Sherwin-Williams* and *Benjamin Moore* are popular commercial paints and are easily purchased if scene paint is not available. The colors on the chart provided here are close approximations of the scene paint colors. Paint samples are available in their stores and in cyberspace. Colors can vary when actually used.

- I am in no way related to the Sherwin-Williams paint company.

Foreword

Everyone has to start somewhere. In the world of illusionist scenic painting, this would be a good place to start. For those of you who have limited class time, this is REALLY the place to start. The notion of handing out the assignment with complete step-by-step instructions during the week before class (so that lengthy demonstrations and explanations do not take up class time) is certainly a noble one. There are certainly many aspects of scenic painting that this book is not very informative about, but the book really gets the students right to the painting activity, leading them through quite a lot of projects and ending with a wonderful group painting that they can all be proud of.

Steve Sherwin is a sensitive and sharp teacher who has come up with flexible solutions to his not-so-unique problems. Like . . . what to do when you need to buy paint from the local paint store, how to build and cover flats for class, how to use existing flats as he uses both units and scale in presenting the projects. What to do with the students who finish first and need extra challenges.

What I like the best is this. He answers many questions before they are asked through the use of partial glossaries, many REALLY USEFUL AND ENLIGHTENING NOTES and "PSs" sprinkled liberally throughout. These explanations really support the idea of "showing them *how* to fish" . . . one of my favorites!

Also, many of the directions are repeated often, probably enough times for them to be noticed.

The computer generated projects that are used (often with zoom insets) aren't high art, but clearly show what is expected. Clarity in this department is surely what is needed as beginners struggle to follow directions.

The student that has gone through this sequence of projects will certainly have manipulated enough paint to know what it feels like. They will have gained proficiency in using many of the techniques often used by Scenic Artists the world over and be ready to use their new understanding of what they are doing to continue toward being a good Scenic Artist.

Rachel Keebler of Cobalt Studios

Acknowledgments

This book would not have been possible without the help and support of many. I wish to thank Greg Roehrick, Western Michigan University, for suggesting the possibilities of a career in scenic design and technical theatre and for assisting my transition from high-school band director to theatre graduate student. I also wish to thank Russell Smith, Wayne State University, who was my first scene painting professor, and Richard Donnelly, Notre Dame, for jump-starting my education in Corel® Painter™.

Thanks to the design and technical theatre faculty at University of Wisconsin–Stevens Point; I can't imagine a finer group of colleagues. Wendy Dolan helped with editing, Gary Olsen suggested this project in the first place, and Susan Sherwin is a brilliant designer and wonderful wife.

Thanks to the Scene Painting Class, Fall 2002 (a.k.a. alpha testers): Casey Adams, Spencer Carlson, Nicholas Fendt, Samantha Fromm, Travis Gaboda, Anthony Galaska, Leah Girtman, Ann Hackbarth, Lacie Hexon, Lori Koeller, Nicole Lemery, Sarah Montross, Mandy Mueller, and Michael Wiskow.

Thanks to the Scene Painting Class, Fall 2004 (a.k.a. beta testers): Amanda Baker, Andrew Bevacqua, Tristan Christ, Rebecca Eske, Rebecca Hengstenberg, Christianna Huber, Kenneth Keith, Sarah Montross, Nathan Rohrer, Jennifer Smith, Sarah Sumnicht, Catherine Tantillo, Rachel Tomsyck, and Michael Wiskow.

Thank you, Rachel Keebler, at Cobalt Studios, for support, suggestions, and a kick in the pants when I needed it the most. Thank you, Cara Anderson, a great editor and advocate.

I had a wonderful family that loved and supported me for many years. Most are not alive, but I often think of them.

Introduction

It's no fun watching paint dry!

University class schedules can be prescriptive. Blocks of time for classes fit a master schedule. Our scene painting course is scheduled for two hours, twice a week. It was difficult presenting and demonstrating a painting project in two hours. I demonstrated on a smaller flat in the middle of the circle of students. The students were expected to take notes, and they did, but the class met in the scene shop, where desks and writing space were at a premium. Progress stopped while paint dried. I'm sure there are multiple solutions to these problems. A book containing painting projects and step-by-step instructions would be the answer to my problems.

I thought there would be many advantages with this type of book. Instructions are in print so note-taking is minimized. Students could review the project and instructions in advance of the class. We would review the instructions and allow for questions during class. The demonstration day would now be a painting day. I would walk around the room and address questions to individuals as they painted. I could stop the class to address common problems and concerns of benefit to the entire class. All I had to do was find this book.

Many theatre design books contain sections or small chapters with painting examples, but there are only a few finished products in color. Books on faux painting, while instructive, are not specifically designed for theatrical production. There are excellent photographic reference books containing pictures of source material; however, I wanted my students to duplicate a painting, not a photograph. There are many excellent resources available to scenic artists, but a book of painting projects was missing from the list. I decided to write this book as a result of my search.

When I prepared a sabbatical proposal with the subject of activities in computers and technology, a colleague suggested that preparing a scene painting manual would be a much better subject for a sabbatical. He was correct.

Additional books cover the role of the scenic artist, the tools and equipment, and techniques for painting. I urge you to add these wonderful books to your library. I hope this book will be their companion.

Stephen G. Sherwin

About This Book

The art, practice, and technique of scene painting is an essential part of theatre design. These skills are mandatory for scenic designers and scenic artists. Costume, lighting, and properties designers also benefit greatly from these techniques and skills. Painting is an essential part of most theatrical productions, either creating the illusion of three dimensions or reinforcing dimensional scenery.

This book is divided into chapters or projects. The first page of every chapter contains an overview of the painting project. It includes information about work surface and the type and consistency of paint. It also reviews the concepts and techniques of the painting project. A partial glossary is provided, as well as a list of tools needed for the project.

The second page of every chapter is a paint elevation. The elevation in a relative scale appears on the right side of the page. Paint color examples are included. The first title of every color swatch refers to the function or purpose of that color (for example, Base, Spatter, Wash). The second title of every color swatch is the color name. This will help students learn and talk about color. The paint colors used in projects are mostly colors "out of the can." The projects try to make paint mixing simple. Difficult color mixing is an advanced skill covered in more advanced books.

The remaining pages of each chapter provide step-by-step examples and include a picture for that particular step. The NOTES section at the bottom of the page includes general information not specifically about the project (most of the time).

Consult the next page for a pictorial example

It is possible that a student or a class will start with project 1 and continue in sequence to the end of the book. It is also likely that projects will be painted out of sequence. It is for this reason that projects contain some repetitive information.

Adapt the projects for individual situations. Many projects, especially toward the end of the book, could be divided into multiple weeks, similar to the Bookshelf/Book projects. The Drapery project could be painted over the Wallpaper project, for example.

As mentioned earlier, one problem with teaching scene painting is waiting for paint to dry. A painting video can edit out drying time, and in production the painting projects are large enough to allow drying time with little break in the painting process. The book should help as much as a book can by illustrating the individual steps of the painting process.

The project number is provided at the top of the page.

The project title is next.

The step number for a specific project is in this area, followed by a short title.

Instructions are in this area and often reference the painted example on the right side of the page.

Instruction steps are contained in a list.

Scale, 2 units wide × 3 units high.

A 4′ × 6′ flat works well.

Titles in **bold** indicate paint names found on the elevation.

IMPORTANT!
- Occasionally, a box like this one will appear in this area. Please read it!

NOTES
- This box contains information more general in nature and helpful in the future.
- **P.S.** Occasionally, you will see a **P.S.** section, which provides suggestions for additional study or research or painting projects for students wanting more experience.

PROJECT 1
Texture Techniques

WORK SURFACE

A 4′ × 6′ traditional or hard-covered flat.

TYPE OF PAINT

Rosco *Off Broadway* paint, Rosco *Iddings Deep Colors*, or a commercial latex substitute. See the COLOR SAMPLES page at the beginning of this book for brand and color suggestions.

TYPES OF CONSISTENCY

OUT OF THE CAN—Rosco suggests that the paint can be used right out of the can. This consistency might be thick. Add water to achieve a NORMAL consistency (see below).

NORMAL—Thick enough just to cover other projects in a single coat, assuming that the difference between the paint colors is not too great.

DILUTED—1 or 2 parts paint to 1 part water added to the NORMAL paint consistency.

WATERY—1 part paint to 5 to 10 parts water added to the NORMAL paint consistency. Rosco says: "Diluting with more than 2 parts water may reduce binder strength. Add Rosco *Clear Acrylic Glaze* to restore adhesion and flexibility."

PAINTING TECHNIQUES

SCUMBLE (paint technique)—Blending two or more random patches of color. Size of the patches and the amount of blend will vary depending on the project.

GRADED WET BLEND (paint technique)—To arrange in a scale or series; a smooth blend of colors using a gradation, usually a linear pattern blended together.

SPONGING (paint technique)—Creating a texture by applying paint with a sponge.

DRY BRUSH (paint technique)—Dragging a brush loaded with paint across a dry surface (also called "combing").

RAG ROLLING (paint technique)—Creating a texture by applying paint with a rolled rag dipped into paint.

ROLLING (paint technique)—Applying color with a paint roller. The texture of the roller cover will show when a dryer roller is used.

SPATTER (paint technique)—A method of texture using a brush to throw drops of paint on a surface.

SPLATTER (paint technique)—A method of texture using a brush to throw a combination of water and drops of paint on a surface (also called "wet spatter").

BATH (paint technique)—A method of texture using a brush to throw a combination of a large quantity of water and drops of paint on a surface.

Glossary

OMNIDIRECTIONAL BRUSH STROKE—Applying paint in a random pattern of brush strokes, usually in a figure-eight configuration. This will leave very little grain in the paint when dry.

KRAFT PAPER—Nonabsorbent paper used to protect against spills and protect scenery from additional paint applications.

PAINT ELEVATIONS

Scale, 2 units wide × 3 units high.

TOOLS NEEDED
(See the Project pages for details.)

- **A collection of scene and housepainting brushes**
- **Chalk or charcoal for cartooning**
- **Tape measure and straightedge**
- **Sponge**
- **Masking tape and Kraft paper**
- **Bucket of clean water**

Texture #1
Sky blue

Texture #2
Sky blue - medium

Texture #3
Sky blue - light

Texture #4
Ultramarine blue

Texture #5
Purple

Texture #6
Emerald green

Texture #7
Chrome oxide green

Texture #8
Black

Scale, 2 units wide × 3 units high.

STEP 1
Two-Color Scumble

Prepare the **Texture #1** and **Texture #3** paint colors used for the scumble base.

- Add a little water to the NORMAL paint consistency. This will help the blending process.
- Divide the flat in half vertically.

Use a 2″ or 3″ brush to paint patches of the two scumble colors.

- Work a smaller area of the flat at a time.
- The patches of color can touch each other but should not blend at this time.
- Either use two brushes or clean the brush out a bit after applying each color.
- Before the paint dries, use a clean brush to blend the colors. Use an omnidirectional brush stroke when blending the colors together.
- Don't overwork the blending. The goal is to have a number of colors as a result of the blending. There should be places where the two colors are not blended at all.

Titles in **bold** indicate paint names found on the elevation.

NOTES

- In terms of time, scumble should take only a little longer than base painting. Scumble should be a quick technique but adds more interest than one color of base paint.

- There are two major factors that affect the look of scumble. One is the number and contrast of the paint colors. The second is the size of the brushes used for the technique.

- Have a bucket of clean water. Although this seems obvious, handy clean water will solve a variety of problems.

STEP 2
Gradient

Prepare the paint used for the graded wet blend (**Texture #1**, **Texture #2**, and **Texture #3**).

- These paints should be NORMAL consistency. (See NOTES.)
- Cover the scumbled half of the flat with Kraft paper.

The purpose of the graded wet blend is to achieve an even progression from one color to another.

- Divide the flat into three horizontal sections.
- Base the top section with **Texture #1**.
- Base the middle section with **Texture #2**.
- Blend these two colors before the paint has a chance to dry.
- Use a clean, damp brush for the blending.
- Work quickly and use a light stroke.

Base the bottom section with **Texture #3**.

- Blend these two colors before the paint has a chance to dry. (See NOTES.)
- Use a clean, damp brush for the blending.
- Work quickly and use a light stroke.
- Don't overwork this technique. (See NOTES.)

Titles in **bold** indicate paint names found on the elevation.

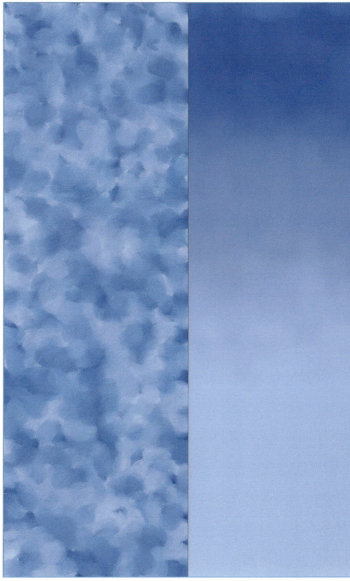

Scale, 2 units wide × 3 units high.

NOTES

- Mixing equal parts of **Texture #1** and **Texture #3** will produce **Texture #2**. When the paint is correctly mixed, place a drop of one color into the other buckets and compare the relationship. A drop of the other colors will not affect the original color of the paint.

- If **Texture #2** is dry when beginning to blend **Texture #2** and **Texture #3**, rebase the bottom of the middle section with **Texture #2**.

- If brush strokes are noticeable and too rough after the blend, smooth out this area. While the paint is still wet, use a clean, damp 4″ brush to gently blend the paint on a horizontal line.

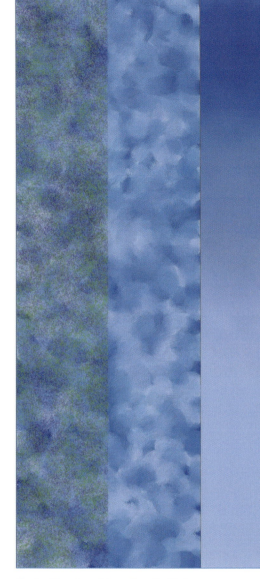

Scale, 2 units wide × 3 units high.

STEP 3
Sponging

Use a natural sponge to paint the first half of the scumbled area.

- Prepare the **Texture #5** and **Texture #6** paint colors.

- The left half of the scumbled area is sponged. Mask the right edge with a piece of Kraft paper.

- After the scumble dries, sponge the left quarter of the flat using these two colors, one at a time.

- Dip the natural sponge in the **Texture #5** paint color and remove the excess. Test the paint on another surface before painting the flat. (See NOTES.)

- When a random texture is desired, as in this project, constantly rotate the sponge to avoid developing a pattern.

- Allow to dry a bit and repeat with **Texture #6**.

Titles in **bold** indicate paint names found on the elevation.

NOTES

- Use a natural sponge for this technique. A small sponge (about 6″ in diameter) will work fine for a small project. Use a large sponge for large areas. They can be expensive and difficult to find, especially in larger sizes.

- The sponge technique should go all the way to the edges of the designated paint area.

- A synthetic sponge will leave a repetitive and predictable pattern. It works well for other techniques but not for this project.

STEP 4
Dry Brush or Combing

Prepare the **Texture #4**, **Texture #7**, and **Texture #1** paint colors.

- Add a little water to the NORMAL paint consistency. This will help the blending process.

- The right half of the scumbled area is dry brushed. Mask the gradient half of the flat and the sponged section with a piece of Kraft paper. Wait for the sponge technique to dry before covering with Kraft paper.

Use a 3″ brush to paint the second half of the scumbled area.

- Load the brush with a minimum of **Texture #4** paint. Lightly press and move the brush over the flat. The scumble base layer should not be completely covered.

- Go as long as possible before lifting the brush or running out of paint. If the brush runs out of paint, lift gradually so as not to see a visible brush line.

- Variation in the dry brush is not desirable in this project. Try to keep the dry brush as straight as possible.

Use a 3″ brush to paint **Texture #7** and **Texture #1**.

- The techniques listed above also apply to this application.

Titles in **bold** indicate paint names found on the elevation.

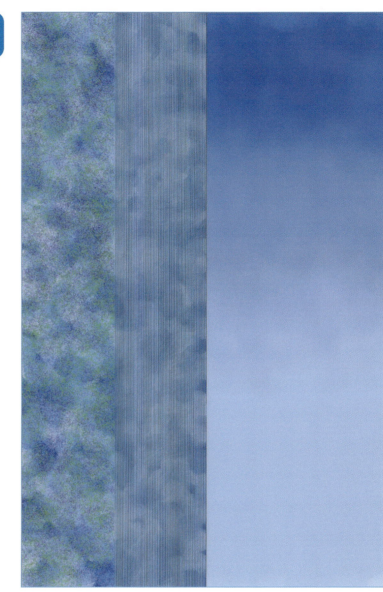

Scale, 2 units wide × 3 units high.

1

NOTES

- A brand new and well cared for brush is not the best choice for the dry brush technique in this project.

- Please take care of paint brushes. Even with proper care, brushes will age and bristles will start to separate. Don't throw away these brushes. They will work very well for this type of dry brush, spattering, and other painting techniques.

- Cut into the bristles of a new and inexpensive brush if an old brush is not available. This technique will ruin the brush for other applications.

- Bristled disposable brushes that are great tools for painting this type of dry brush technique are also available.

Things to Remember

1

STEP 5
Rag Rolling

Mix the **Texture #5** and **Texture #2** paint colors.

- Add a little water to the NORMAL paint consistency. This will help the blending process.

- The left half of the gradient area is rag rolled. Mask the scumbled half of the flat and the right gradient section with a piece of Kraft paper. Wait for the dry brush technique to dry before covering with Kraft paper.

There are a number of approaches for a rag-rolling technique:

- Find a rag suitable for painting. Bunch up the rag. It should be about the same size as a paint roller. Wet the rag with water and wring out excess water. Dip the rag in paint and remove the excess. Lay the rag on the area to be painted and roll the rag until it is out of paint. This technique works best when the flat is horizontal. (See NOTES.)

- Find a rag suitable for painting. Wrap the rag loosely around a paint roller. Tie the ends and a few places in the middle with string. Dip the rag in paint and roll out the excess. Lay the rag roller on the area to be painted and roll until it is out of paint. This technique works when the surface is horizontal or vertical. (See NOTES.)

Titles in **bold** indicate paint names found on the elevation.

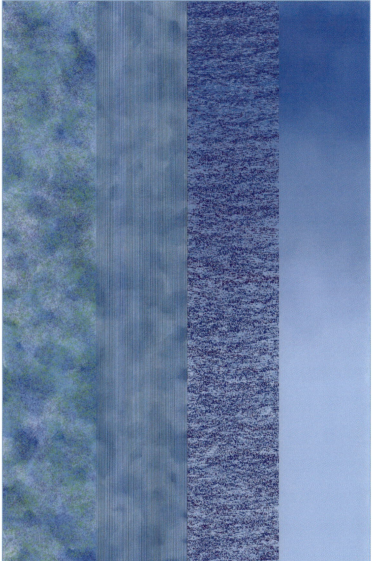

Scale, 2 units wide × 3 units high.

NOTES
- Begin to notice the variations in the combined techniques. The twelve areas on the flat will all finish with three different painting techniques. It is interesting to see the results of multiple and varied techniques.

- Experiment on a test flat. This flat is usually a small flat (maybe 2′ × 3′) constructed and prepared like the finished flat. IT IS VERY IMPORTANT TO USE A TEST FLAT! This technique requires practice, and the finished flat will make a bad test flat.

- The ability to paint with a broom handle and the rag-covered roller is an advantage of this technique when painting larger areas.

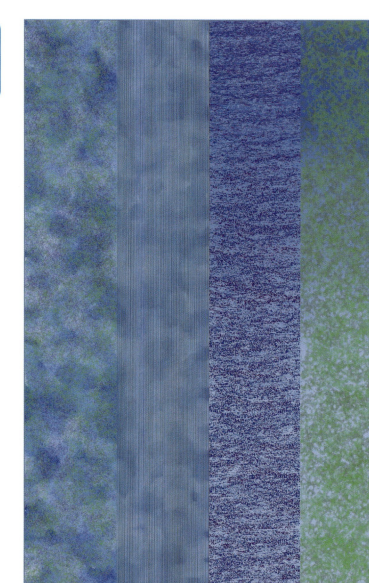

Scale, 2 units wide × 3 units high.

STEP 6
Roller

Prepare the **Texture #6** and **Texture #7** paint colors.

- Add a little water to the NORMAL paint consistency. This will help the blending process.

- The right half of the gradient area is rolled. Mask the left gradient section with a piece of Kraft paper. Wait for the rag-rolled technique to dry before covering with Kraft paper.

Using a roller for texture is a fairly simple technique. (See NOTES.)

- A new roller cover works best for this technique. The pile on an old roller cover is too worn for this technique.

- Dip the roller in paint and roll out the excess. It is important to evenly distribute the paint around the roller. Lay the roller on the area to be painted and roll until it is out of paint. A light touch is necessary for this technique. (See NOTES.)

- Don't forget to clean the roller cover between colors.

Titles in **bold** indicate paint names found on the elevation.

NOTES

- An old tray is ideal for holding paint and loading rollers when the roller is used for texture and not base painting. A small amount of paint is all that is needed, and the tray fits that purpose. When an accident happens (such as a person stepping on the tray), the mess is more manageable to clean up and less paint is wasted.

- Experiment on a test flat. This technique is not difficult, but it is important to use a minimum of paint to avoid lines created by the ends of the roller.

STEP 7
Spatter

Prepare the **Texture #8** paint color. (See NOTES.)

- The paint should be the DILUTED consistency. This is important. Proper consistency will help the spatter process. (See NOTES.)

- The top third of the flat is spattered. Mask the middle and bottom thirds with Kraft paper.

Use a 3″ or 4″ brush to paint the spatter. This is a good time to use an old brush that might not be good for anything else.

- Dip the brush in the paint and use the side of the bucket to remove excess paint from the brush, then swipe the brush on the floor or other approved area to remove even more excess.

- For this project, start off the flat and move over it. Any blobs of paint still in the brush will discharge before they get to the flat. (See NOTES.)

Titles in **bold** indicate paint names found on the elevation.

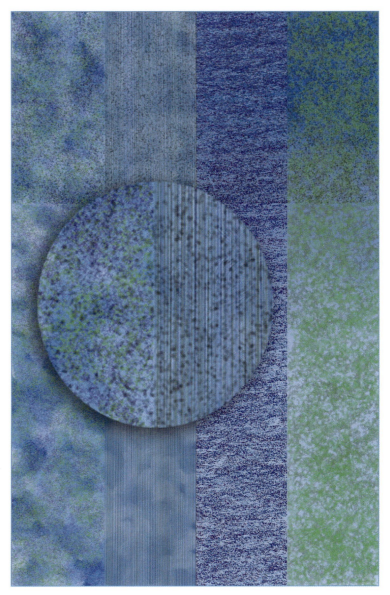

Scale, 2 units wide × 3 units high.

NOTES

- The consistency of the spatter paint should be DILUTED. If the paint is too thick, it will stay on the brush. If the paint is too thin, it will not read very well on the finished flat.

- There are many ways of applying spatter. One method is to hit the spatter brush against a stick or hand to control the application. Flicking the wrist in the direction of the painting surface but avoiding back-snap is another possibility. Wildly swinging the brush is likely to deposit paint on all adjacent surfaces, including coworkers. This will make the supervisors upset.

- This is a small area to spatter. A sprayer can be used for larger projects.

Scale, 2 units wide × 3 units high.

STEP 8
Splatter (Spatter with Additional Water)

Prepare the **Texture #8** paint color.

- The paint should be the DILUTED consistency. This is important. Proper consistency will help with the application process.

- The middle third of the flat is splattered. Mask the top and bottom thirds with Kraft paper.

- Make sure the previous paint application is completely dry before painting this step.

Use a 3″ or 4″ brush to paint the splatter. This is a good time to use an old brush that might not be good for anything else.

- Use less paint with more water for splattering. (See NOTES.)

- Either splatter the paint directly on the flat or splatter clean water on the flat before the paint splatter is applied.

- Water with less pigment may be used for splatter (wet spatter) and will not require the additional water application. Please test the mixing and application of splatter. Allow the paint to dry for a true test of the final results.

- This technique is also called "wet spatter."

Titles in **bold** indicate paint names found on the elevation.

NOTES

- There is one letter difference between the words *splatter* and *spatter*. Make sure the technique being communicated is correct. The painting techniques are similar. Think of splatter as spatter with additional water. Splatter can also be called "wet spatter."

- Have a bucket of clear water handy when splattering. If the splatter wash is too heavy and defined, splatter clean water to help diffuse and blend the paint.

- Have a sponge handy to absorb any excess or unwanted water.

STEP 9
Bath (Splatter with Additional Water)

Mix the **Texture #8** paint color.

- The paint should be the DILUTED consistency. This is important. Proper consistency will help with the application process.

- The bottom third of the flat is splattered. Mask the top and middle thirds with Kraft paper.

- Make sure the previous paint application is completely dry before painting this step.

Use a 3″ or 4″ brush to paint the splatter. This is a good time to use an old brush that might not be good for anything else.

- Use more water than used for splattering (wet spatter).

- Apply clean water on the flat before the paint splatter is applied.

- Watch the application very carefully. Even with the top and middle masked, water can seep under the material used for masking. Tip the flat ever so slightly to prevent the water from running on the middle splatter.

Titles in **bold** indicate paint names found on the elevation.

Scale, 2 units wide × 3 units high.

NOTES

There are additional popular painting techniques not covered in this project:

- Applying paint with all manner of sprayers

- Flogging

- Using foam stamps, usually shop-built

- Textured rollers, either purchased or shop-built

- Schlepitchka, which is applying paint with a feather duster

All of these techniques will require additional equipment, some expensive. Practice manufacturing a few of these tools and use them on this project.

PROJECT 2
Spattered and Sponged Wall

WORK SURFACE

A 4′ × 6′ traditional or hard-covered flat.

TYPE OF PAINT

Rosco *Off Broadway* paint, Rosco *Iddings Deep Colors*, or a commercial latex substitute. See the COLOR SAMPLES page at the beginning of this book for brand and color suggestions.

TYPES OF CONSISTENCY

OUT OF THE CAN—Rosco suggests that the paint can be used right out of the can. This consistency might be thick. Add water to achieve a NORMAL consistency (see below).

NORMAL—Thick enough just to cover other projects in a single coat, assuming that the difference between the paint colors is not too great.

DILUTED—1 or 2 parts paint to 1 part water added to the NORMAL paint consistency.

WATERY—1 part paint to 5 to 10 parts water added to the NORMAL paint consistency. Rosco says: "Diluting with more than 2 parts water may reduce binder strength. Add Rosco *Clear Acrylic Glaze* to restore adhesion and flexibility."

PAINTING TECHNIQUES

BASE PAINT (paint technique)—The first paint color or colors used in a specific painting project, usually the predominant color.

SPATTER (paint technique)—A method of texture using a brush to throw drops of paint on a surface.

SPONGING (paint technique)—Creating a texture by applying paint with a sponge.

HIGHLIGHT WASH (paint technique)—A light, translucent paint used to represent the reflection of light or an area that receives the greatest amount of illumination.

SHADOW WASH (paint technique)—A dark, transparent paint used to suggest a shadow cast from one object on another.

Glossary

PAINT ELEVATION—A scaled, color drawing or painting of a piece of scenery provided by the scenic designer.

CARTOON—A line drawing of a paint elevation used as a guide for a painting project.

PARTS OF A BRUSH—Handle, ferrule (the metal band that holds the bristles), and bristles.

HOLIDAY—Part of a surface unintentionally left unpainted.

OMNIDIRECTIONAL BRUSH STROKE—Applying paint in a random pattern of brush strokes, usually in a figure-eight configuration; this will leave very little grain in the paint when dry.

CHAIR RAIL—Horizontal wall trim approximately the height of the top of a chair; used to protect plastered walls from damage caused by the backs of chairs.

BASEBOARD—Molding attached to the bottom of a wall covering the joint of a wall and the adjoining floor.

BEVEL—A sloping part or surface.

Scale, 2 units wide × 3 units high.

TOOLS NEEDED
(See the Project pages for details.)

- **A collection of scene and housepainting brushes**
- **Chalk or charcoal for cartooning**
- **Tape measure and straightedge**
- **Sponge**
- **Bucket of clean water**

Base Chrome oxide green - light	**Sponge base** Raw umber - light	**Medium trim** Raw umber - medium light
Spatter #1 Burnt sienna	**Sponge #1** Raw sienna	**Highlight wash** White/raw umber - 10% opacity
Spatter #2 Pthalo blue	**Sponge #2** Yellow ochre	**Shadow wash** Black/violet - 10% opacity
Spatter #3 Raw umber	**Sponge #3** Burnt sienna - light	

STEP 1
Base the Flat

Base paint the flat with the **Base**.

- If this flat has been used, the paint should be just thick enough to cover the previous painting project.

- If this is a new flat, the paint should be just thick enough to cover the flat.

- In either case, remember that a lot of additional paint will go on this flat. Only a small amount of paint is needed.

- Dip the brush in a small amount of paint. Remember to use the tips of the brush.

- Use a omnidirectional brush stroke when base painting.

- Avoid holidays.

Titles in **bold** indicate paint names found on the elevation.

NOTES

- Scene painting brushes are expensive, aren't they? Always leave enough time at the end of a painting session for proper cleanup, especially brushes.

- Don't soak paint brushes. Soaking can cause bristles to droop, ferrules to rust, and handles to swell.

- Use lukewarm water and a mild soap to clean brushes.

- A wire brush can harm the bristles and even pull them out from the ferrule. Use a brush comb specifically intended for fine brushes.

- Place the brush back in its plastic keeper. If the brush didn't come in one, use a piece of paper towel to gently wrap the bristles.

STEP 2
Spatter

Prepare **Spatter #1**, **Spatter #2**, and **Spatter #3**. (See NOTES.)

- The consistency is important. Proper consistency will help the spatter process.

Use a 3″ or 4″ brush to paint the spatter. This is a good time to use an old brush that might not be good for anything else.

- Start painting with **Spatter #1**.

- Dip the brush in the paint and use the side of the bucket to remove excess paint from the brush, then swipe the brush on the floor or other approved area to remove even more excess.

- For this project, start at the bottom of the flat. Be aware that if there are any blobs of paint still in the brush this area will later be covered with the sponge base during Step 3.

- The spatter can be a little heavier on the top part of the flat. (See NOTES.)

- Repeat the process with **Spatter #2** and **Spatter #3**.

- The last and fourth spatter should be the **Base** paint color. This will help blend the other spatter and will break up areas where the spatter might be too heavy. (Add additional water to the base when using it for spatter.)

Titles in **bold** indicate paint names found on the elevation.

Scale, 2 units wide × 3 units high.

NOTES

- The consistency of the spatter paint should be between a normal paint and a wash. If the paint is too thick, it will stay on the brush. If the paint is too thin, it will not read very well on the finished flat.

- There are many ways of applying spatter. One method is to hit the spatter brush against a stick or hand to control the application. Flicking the wrist in the direction of the painting surface but avoiding back-snap is another possibility. Wildly swinging the brush is likely to deposit paint on all adjacent surfaces, including coworkers. This will make the supervisors upset.

- A heavier and darker concentration of spatter at the top of a full-sized flat is a simple technique to draw less attention to that portion of the wall.

2

Scale, 2 units wide × 3 units high.

STEP 3
Base Paint the Area
for Painting the
Sponge Technique

Locate the dividing line.

- Measure up from the bottom 2′6″ and put a small mark on the side edges of the flat.

- Use these marks and a straightedge to draw a line at the top of the sponged area. (See NOTES.)

- Please measure very carefully. Many projects are ruined because of mistakes made in measurement.

Paint the sponged area.

- Paint the **Sponge base** paint color with a brush. Use a straightedge as a guide to avoid painting over the cartooned line.

- Now use the **Sponge base** paint color to paint below that line.

- Avoid the use of masking or painter's tape when painting this area. Applying tape is time consuming and paint might pull off when the tape is removed.

Titles in **bold** indicate paint names found on the elevation.

NOTES
- When cartooning a flat, use chalk or other light-color material on dark surfaces.

- When cartooning a flat, use vine charcoal or other dark material on light surfaces.

- Make sure that whatever is used can be removed or covered up when paint lines are no longer needed.

- Remember, some materials (such as marker) will not always cover with paint. This might be a problem with the current project and might be a real problem when moving to the next project.

STEP 4
Sponge

Mix **Sponge #1**, **Sponge #2**, and **Sponge #3**.

- After the **Sponge base** dries, sponge the lower part of the flat using these three colors, one at a time.

- The applied paint should be less than 1-1/2″ from the spattered wall but not on the spattered wall. This area will be re-based for the trim.

- Dip the natural sponge in **Sponge #1** and remove the excess. Test the paint on another surface before painting the flat. (See NOTES.)

- When a random texture is desired as in this project, constantly rotate the sponge to avoid developing a pattern.

- Allow to dry a bit and repeat with **Sponge #2**.

- Allow to dry a bit and repeat with **Sponge #3**.

- The last and fourth sponge should be the **Sponge base** paint color. This will help blend the other sponge colors and will break up areas where the sponging might be too heavy. This step is not necessary if the previous sponge colors are even.

Titles in **bold** indicate paint names found on the elevation.

Scale, 2 units wide × 3 units high.

NOTES
- Use a natural sponge for this technique. A small sponge (about 6″ in diameter) will work fine for a small project. Use a large sponge for large areas.

- The sponge technique should go all the way to the edges of the designated paint area.

- A synthetic sponge will leave a repetitive and predictable pattern. It works well for other techniques but not for this project.

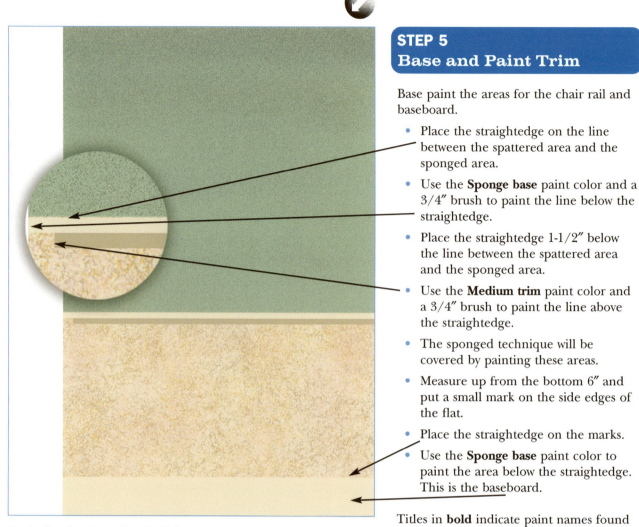

Scale, 2 units wide × 3 units high.

STEP 5
Base and Paint Trim

Base paint the areas for the chair rail and baseboard.

- Place the straightedge on the line between the spattered area and the sponged area.

- Use the **Sponge base** paint color and a 3/4″ brush to paint the line below the straightedge.

- Place the straightedge 1-1/2″ below the line between the spattered area and the sponged area.

- Use the **Medium trim** paint color and a 3/4″ brush to paint the line above the straightedge.

- The sponged technique will be covered by painting these areas.

- Measure up from the bottom 6″ and put a small mark on the side edges of the flat.

- Place the straightedge on the marks.

- Use the **Sponge base** paint color to paint the area below the straightedge. This is the baseboard.

Titles in **bold** indicate paint names found on the elevation.

NOTES
- **Always use a straightedge for painting straight lines.** With this simple sentence, the crusade for straight-line painting begins. This statement will appear in following chapters. On occasion, the sentence will simply be copied from one project to the next. At times, humor might be attempted. The reason is simple. Using a straightedge will save time and improve the look when painting straight lines. Students often paint many projects before discovering this truth.

STEP 6
Highlight and Shadow

Paint the beveled edges of the chair rail and baseboard at the left side of the flat.

- Paint the trim profile with **Medium trim** and a small brush.

- This represents the side view of the trim pieces and should provide visual information on dimension.

Paint the highlights with the **Highlight wash** paint color.

- Paint a sharp highlight at the top of the chair rail.

- Paint a 3/4″ highlight at the top of the baseboard (this is the angled part of the trim and the surface most direct to the light source).

Paint the shadows with the **Shadow wash** paint color.

- Paint a 1″ cast shadow under the chair rail. A small bit should overlap the bottom of the chair rail. This will read as an additional thickness.

- Paint a sharp cutline at the bottom of the chair rail and the top of the baseboard. This will help to separate the trim from the wall. IMPORTANT! These lines are very subtle and are barely seen. Be very careful not to make them too big or too dark. (See NOTES.)

- Use a straightedge for all these lines.

Titles in **bold** indicate paint names found on the elevation.

Scale, 2 units wide × 3 units high.

NOTES

- The shadow cutline should be the same color as the shadow wash. Rather than mix a new color or consistency, use a bit of the shadow wash that settled in the bottom of the container. Please test this paint before applying to the flat.

- **P.S.** The items that might be added to this project are included in the next project.

Distressed Wall with Wainscot

WORK SURFACE

A 4′ × 6′ traditional or hard-covered flat.

TYPE OF PAINT

Rosco *Off Broadway* paint, Rosco *Iddings Deep Colors*, or a commercial latex substitute. See the COLOR SAMPLES page at the beginning of this book for brand and color suggestions.

TYPES OF CONSISTENCY

OUT OF THE CAN—Rosco suggests that the paint can be used right out of the can. This consistency might be thick. Add water to achieve a NORMAL consistency (see below).

NORMAL—Thick enough just to cover other projects in a single coat, assuming that the difference between the paint colors is not too great.

DILUTED—1 or 2 parts paint to 1 part water added to the NORMAL paint consistency.

WATERY—1 part paint to 5 to 10 parts water added to the NORMAL paint consistency. Rosco says: "Diluting with more than 2 parts water may reduce binder strength. Add Rosco *Clear Acrylic Glaze* to restore adhesion and flexibility."

PAINTING TECHNIQUES

BASE PAINT (paint technique)—The first paint color or colors used in a specific painting project, usually the predominant color.

SPATTER (paint technique)—A method of texture using a brush to throw drops of paint on a surface.

SPLATTER (paint technique)—A method of texture using a brush to throw a combination of water and drops of paint on a surface (also called "wet spatter").

GRAINING (paint technique)—Creating a texture by dry brushing or combing to achieve a naturally formed pattern found in wood or marble.

DISTRESSING—To mar deliberately to give an effect of age.

CARTOON—A line drawing of a paint elevation used as a guide for a painting project.

HIGHLIGHT WASH (paint technique)—A light, translucent paint used to represent the reflection of light or an area that receives the greatest amount of illumination.

SHADOW WASH (paint technique)—A dark, transparent paint used to suggest a shadow cast from one object on another.

Glossary

LATH—A rough strip of wood fastened to studs as a base for plaster.

WAINSCOT—The lower three or four feet (about one meter) of an interior wall finished differently from the remainder of the wall; usually vertical trim.

CHAIR RAIL—Horizontal wall trim approximately the height of the top of a chair; used to protect plastered walls from damage caused by the backs of chairs.

BASEBOARD—Molding attached to the bottom of a wall covering the joint of a wall and the adjoining floor.

Scale, 2 units wide × 3 units high.

LIGHT DIRECTION

TOOLS NEEDED
(See the Project pages for details.)

- **A collection of scene and housepainting brushes**

- **Chalk or charcoal for cartooning**

- **Tape measure**

- **Straightedge or lining stick**

- **A small brush, feather, or razor striper for painting cracks**

Base
Chrome oxide green - light

Wash #1
Black/violet - 10% opacity

Wash #2
Raw sienna - 10% opacity

Wood base
Raw sienna

Wood grain #1
Burnt sienna

Wood grain #2
Raw umber

Wood grain #3
Black - 50% opacity

Highlight wash
White/raw sienna - 10% opacity

Scale, 2 units wide × 3 units high.

STEP 1
Wall Distressing, Part One

Splatter the flat for a distressed look. (See NOTES.)

- Mix **Wash #1** with additional water. Use this paint to splatter the flat. Use less paint with more water for splattering. (See NOTES.)

- The effect of splatter in this project will add age and dirt to the wall. The goal is to apply the splatter in an uneven pattern.

- Either splatter the paint directly on the flat or splatter clear water on the flat before the paint splatter is applied.

- Paint with less pigment used for splatter might not require the water application. Please test the mixing and application of splatter; allow to dry for a true test.

- Repeat the technique with **Wash #2**.

- Some of the wash will fall on the sponge and trim from the previous project.

Paint the cracks.

- Paint the cracks with **Wood grain #2** and additional water. (See NOTES.)

- Real cracks in walls are irregular, random, and difficult to see. Use restraint when painting cracks.

- Using a small amount of highlight and shadow wash will give the crack line dimension. Remember the direction of the light.

Titles in **bold** indicate paint names found on the elevation.

NOTES

- There is one letter difference between the words *splatter* and *spatter*. Make sure the technique being communicated is correct. The painting techniques are similar. Think of splatter as spatter with additional water.

- Have a bucket of clear water handy when splattering. If the splatter wash is too heavy and defined, splatter clean water to help diffuse and blend the paint.

- A small brush, feather, or razor striper will work well for painting the cracks. This is a very loose and shaky technique.

3

Things to Remember

Scale, 2 units wide × 3 units high.

3

STEP 2
Wall Distressing, Part Two

Paint the exposed lath at the top.

- Cartoon the area that will be the exposed lathe with chalk or charcoal.

- Base this area with the **Wood base**.

- Dry brush the lathe planks between the cracks with **Wood grain #1**.

- Repeat the dry brush, this time with **Wood grain #2**.

- Use **Wood grain #3** to paint the space between each lathe. These lines will appear random if they are painted without a straightedge.

- Use **Wash #1** and **Highlight wash** to give the cracked plaster dimension. Remember the direction of the light.

- Paint a narrow shadow at the bottom of each lathe.

Paint picture shadows.

- Pictures hung on the wall leave a relatively clean area when they are removed.

- Use spatter to create the appearance of dirt around the pictures.

- Make a template the proper size. (See NOTES.)

- Spatter **Wash #1** around the templates. Take care, as only a small amount of spatter is needed. Add more spatter if necessary. (See NOTES.)

Titles in **bold** indicate paint names found on the elevation.

NOTES

- The stained area represents the space on the wall where a picture was hanging. Measure that size. Cut two pieces of scrap plywood, cardboard, or Kraft paper to that size. If using paper, weight it down before painting.

- Control the spatter that implies the dirt around removed pictures. Hit the spatter brush against a stick or hand to control the application.

STEP 3
Base and Cartoon the Wainscot

Base paint the flat with the **Wood base**.

- Dip the brush in a small amount of paint. Remember to use the tips of the brush.
- Use an omnidirectional brush stroke when base painting.
- Take care to paint within the lines.
- Avoid holidays.

Use chalk or charcoal to cartoon the flat.

- Please measure very carefully.
- Many projects are ruined because of mistakes made in measurement.
- Consider delaying the cartooning of the trim until after the wainscot is painted.

Titles in **bold** indicate paint names found on the elevation.

Scale, 2 units wide × 3 units high.

IMPORTANT!

It is vital that the wood grain painting goes all the way to the edges of the area.

- Consider first painting the dry brush on the wainscot area.
- Re-base the baseboard and chair rail area when dry.
- When the base is dry, dry brush the baseboard and chair rail area.
- Refer to the next two pages for details.

3

NOTES

- When cartooning a flat, use chalk or other light-color material on dark surfaces.

- When cartooning a flat, use vine charcoal or other dark material on light surfaces.

- Make sure that whatever is used can be removed or covered up with paint when the guides are no longer needed.

- Remember, some materials (such as marker) will not always cover with paint. This might be a problem with the current project and might be a real problem when moving to the next project.

Things to Remember

STEP 4
Dry Brush the Wainscot and Base the Trim

Use a 3″ brush to paint **Wood grain #1**.

- The consistency of the paint should have a little more water than is normal.

- Load the brush with a minimum of paint. Lightly press and move the brush over the flat. The **Wood base** should not completely cover.

- Variation in the dry brush is desirable. Roll the brush when painting a plank or rotate the brush from side to side while keeping the bristles flat against the surface. Either method will achieve variation in the brush stroke.

Use a 3″ brush to paint **Wood grain #2** and **Wood grain #3**.

- The techniques previously explained also apply to this application.

Use **Wood grain #3** to paint a small separation line between the planks of the wainscot.

- Use a straightedge to paint this line.

- This is a narrow line.

- A perfect, consistent line is not the desired effect. There is one chance to paint this line. If the paint skips some places it's all right, even desirable.

Use **Wood base** to paint the baseboard and chair rail areas.

Titles in **bold** indicate paint names found on the elevation.

Scale, 2 units wide × 3 units high.

3

> **NOTES**
>
> - A brand new and well cared for brush is not the best choice for the dry brush technique in this project.
>
> - Please take care of brushes. Even with proper care, brushes will age and bristles will begin to separate. Don't throw away these brushes. They will work very well for this type of dry brush, spattering, and other painting techniques.
>
> - If an old brush is not available, consider hacking up a new and inexpensive brush.
>
> - Bristled disposable brushes are my favorite tools for painting this type of dry brush technique.

Things to Remember

STEP 5
Paint the Trim

Use a 3″ brush to paint **Wood grain #1** on the baseboard.

- The consistency of the paint should have a little more water than is normal.

- Load the brush with a minimum of paint. Lightly press and move the brush over the flat. The **Wood base** should not completely cover.

- Variation in the dry brush is desirable. Roll the brush when painting a plank or rotate the brush from side to side while keeping the bristles flat against the surface. Either method will achieve variation in the brush stroke.

Use a 3″ brush to paint **Wood grain #2** and **Wood grain #3** on the baseboard.

- The techniques previously explained also apply to this application.

Use a smaller brush to repeat the dry brush process on the chair rail.

Titles in **bold** indicate paint names found on the elevation.

Scale, 2 units wide × 3 units high.

NOTES
- Always use a straightedge for painting straight lines.

- "I can paint a straight line without a straightedge" or "It takes too long to paint and move a straightedge" or "It looks just fine without using a straightedge" are just a few of the excuses for not using a straightedge that are heard on a regular basis. All of these excuses are invalid!

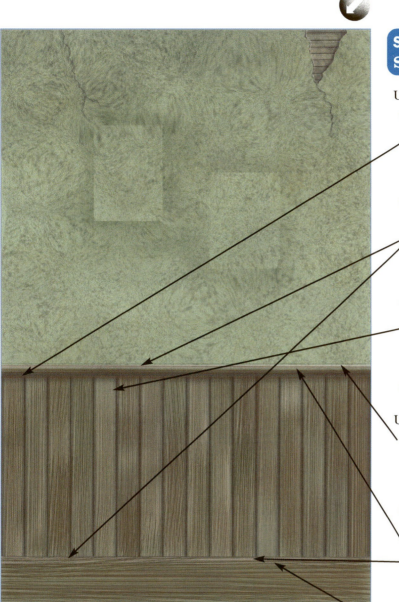

Scale, 2 units wide × 3 units high.

STEP 6
Shadow and Highlight

Use the **Shadow wash** to paint:

- Paint a 1″ cast shadow below the chair rail using the shadow wash. A small bit should overlap the bottom of the chair rail. This will read as an additional thickness.

- Paint a sharp shadow line at the top of the chair rail and the baseboard. This will help to separate the trim from the wall. It is very important that this line be very narrow and not very noticeable.

- Paint a 1/4″ shadow in the space between the planks. A small bit should overlap the sides of each plank. This will appear as a "V" groove between planks.

- Use a straightedge for all of these lines.

Use the **Highlight wash** to paint.

- Paint a sharp highlight on the top of the chair rail. This is the sharp edge of the trim illuminated by the light source.

- Paint a 1/2″ wide highlight at the top of the chair rail and a 3/4″ wide highlight at the top of the baseboard. This is the angled part of the trim and the surface most direct to the light source.

- Paint a sharp highlight on the baseboard 3/4″ from the top. This is the sharp edge of the trim illuminated by the light source.

- Use a straightedge for all these lines.

Titles in **bold** indicate paint names found on the elevation.

NOTES
- The bright edge reflection should be the same color as the highlight wash. Rather than mix a new color or consistency, use a bit of the highlight wash that has settled in the bottom of the container.

- The same is true for the sharp shadow line.

STEP 7
Final Distressing

Splatter the wainscot for a distressed look.

- The wall and the wainscot should have the same dirty look.

- Add additional water to **Wash #1**. Use this paint to splatter the wainscot. Use less paint with more water than used for splattering. (See NOTES.)

- The effect of splatter in this project will add age and dirt to the wall. The goal is to apply the splatter in an uneven pattern.

- Either splatter the paint directly on the flat or splatter clear water on the flat before the paint splatter is applied.

- Splatter paint with a small amount of pigment might not require the water application before the splatter is applied.

- Please test the mixing and application of splatter; allow it to dry for a true test.

- Repeat the technique with **Wash #2**.

Titles in **bold** indicate paint names found on the elevation.

Scale, 2 units wide × 3 units high.

NOTES
- Have a bucket of clean water handy when splattering. If the splatter wash is too heavy and defined, splatter clean water to help diffuse and blend the paint.

- **P.S.** There is no end to the amount of dirt, filth, and degradation that could be added to the flat. Consider adding additional distressing.

PROJECT 4
Wall with Beveled Block

WORK SURFACE

A 4′ × 6′ traditional or hard-covered flat.

TYPE OF PAINT

Rosco *Off Broadway* paint, Rosco *Iddings Deep Colors*, or a commercial latex substitute. See the COLOR SAMPLES page at the beginning of this book for brand and color suggestions.

TYPES OF CONSISTENCY

OUT OF THE CAN—Rosco suggests that the paint can be used right out of the can. This consistency might be thick. Add water to achieve a NORMAL consistency (see below).

NORMAL—Thick enough just to cover other projects in a single coat, assuming that the difference between the paint colors is not too great.

DILUTED—1 or 2 parts paint to 1 part water added to the NORMAL paint consistency.

WATERY—1 part paint to 5 to 10 parts water added to the NORMAL paint consistency. Rosco says: "Diluting with more than 2 parts water may reduce binder strength. Add Rosco *Clear Acrylic Glaze* to restore adhesion and flexibility."

PAINTING TECHNIQUES

SCUMBLE (paint technique)—Blending two or more random patches of color. Size of the patches and the amount of blend will vary depending on the project.

CARTOON—A line drawing of a paint elevation used as a guide for a painting project.

SHADOW WASH (paint technique)—A dark, transparent paint used to suggest a shadow cast from one object on another.

HIGHLIGHT WASH (paint technique)—A light, translucent paint used to represent the reflection of light or an area that receives the greatest amount of illumination.

CUTLINE (paint technique)—Small detail lines that help to differentiate edges and planes.

Glossary

OMNIDIRECTIONAL BRUSH STROKE—applying paint in a random pattern of brush strokes, usually in a figure-eight configuration. This will leave very little grain in the paint when dry.

BLOCK (CINDER)—A hollow rectangular building block made of cement and coal cinders.

BEVEL—A sloping part or surface.

STRAIGHTEDGE—A straight length of wood with a handle that ensures the painting of a straight line.

MORTAR—A building material; usually a mixture of cement, lime, or gypsum plaster with sand and water that hardens and is used in masonry to connect bricks or blocks.

FLAT-FERRULE BRUSH—A wide-width and narrow-edged brush commonly used for housepainting.

SASH BRUSH—A flat-ferrule brush with bristles trimmed on an angle.

SCENIC FITCH—A scenic brush with a long, wooden handle and an oval-shaped ferrule.

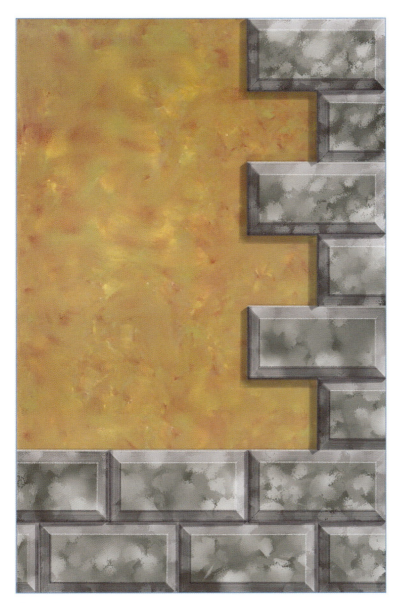

Scale, 2 units wide × 3 units high.

TOOLS NEEDED
(See the Project pages for details.)

- **A collection of scene and housepainting brushes**
- **Chalk or charcoal for cartooning**
- **Tape measure**
- **Straightedge**
- **Bucket of clean water**

Wall scumble #1
Raw Sienna

Wall scumble #2
Burnt Sienna

Wall scumble #3
Yellow Ochre

Block scumble #1
Cool gray - dark

Block scumble #2
Cool gray - medium

Block scumble #3
Cool gray - light

Shadow wash
Black/violet - 10% opacity

Highlight wash
Light gray/violet - 10% opacity

Dark liner
Black/violet - 50% opacity

Light liner
White/violet - 50% opacity

Scale, 2 units wide × 3 units high.

STEP 1
Scumble the Background Wall Texture

Prepare **Wall scumble #1**, **Wall scumble #2**, and **Wall scumble #3** for the scumble base.

- Add a small amount of water to the NORMAL consistency paint. This will help the blending process.

Use a 2″ or 3″ brush to paint patches of all three scumble colors.

- Work a quarter of the flat at a time.
- The patches of color can touch each other but should not blend at this time. (See the insert at the bottom of the elevation.)
- Either use three brushes or clean the brush out a bit after applying each color.
- The quantity of **Wall scumble #2** on the flat should be less than the other two scumble colors; otherwise, the burnt sienna could dominate the raw sienna and yellow ochre.
- Before the paint dries, use a clean brush to blend the colors. Use an omnidirectional brush stroke when blending the colors together.
- Don't overwork the blending. The goal is to have a number of colors as a result of the blending. There should be places where the three colors are not blended at all.

Titles in **bold** indicate paint names found on the elevation.

NOTES
- Don't bother measuring for the blocks on the right of the flat. It will take longer to measure and paint to the edge than it will to simply scumble the entire area and lay the blocks in on the next step.

- In terms of time, scumble should take only a little longer than base painting. Scumble should be a quick technique, but it adds more interest than one color of base paint.

- Now would be a great time to scumble a test flat.

STEP 2
Cartoon the Block

Use chalk or charcoal to cartoon the outline of the architectural beveled block.

- Please measure very carefully. Take time to avoid mistakes.

- Many projects are less than successful because of mistakes made in measurement.

- Blocks measure 18″ in length by 9″ in height.

- There in no need to cartoon the bevel at this time, as it will be covered with the scumble block.

Titles in **bold** indicate paint names found on the elevation.

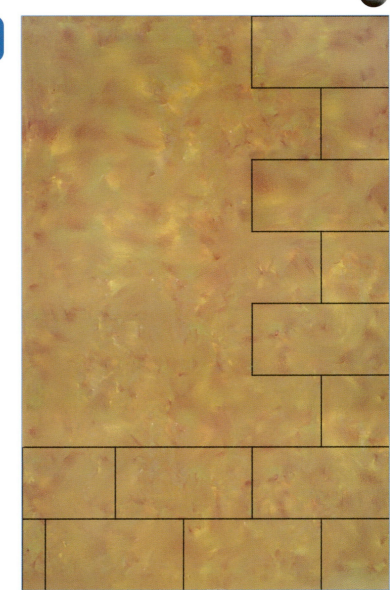

Scale, 2 units wide × 3 units high.

NOTES
- It is important to test and practice the color and painting techniques before applying them to the final project.

- A test surface is highly recommended.

- A test flat, approximately 2′ × 3′, will work well for testing paint. It is lighter weight than a solid piece of wood and is made from the same materials.

- Base the test flat at the same time the project flat is based.

Scale, 2 units wide × 3 units high.

STEP 3
Scumble the Block

Mix **Block scumble #1**, **Block scumble #2**, and **Block scumble #3** for the scumble base.

- Using the NORMAL paint consistency with a small amount of additional water will help the blending process.

- Mix **Block scumble #1**, the cool gray/dark paint color. Divide this paint in half. Add white to one half to get **Block scumble #2**. Put a third of this paint in another bucket and add white to get **Block scumble #3**. (See NOTES.)

- Mix a small amount of paint.

Use a 2″ or 3″ brush to paint patches of all three scumble colors.

- Work one block at a time. Take care to stay in the lines.

- The patches of color can touch each other but should not blend at this time.

- Use three brushes, or clean the brush out a bit after applying each color.

- Before the paint dries, use a clean brush to blend the colors. Use an omnidirectional brush stroke when blending the colors together.

- Don't overwork the blending. The goal is to have a number of colors as a result of the blending. There should be places where the three colors are not blended at all.

Titles in **bold** indicate paint names found on the elevation.

NOTES
- When the paint is correctly mixed, place a drop of one color into the other buckets and compare the relationship. A drop of the other colors will not affect the original color of the paint.

- Consider the use of masking for this step in the project. Masking is not needed if the scumble technique is fairly precise. Remember that mortar and cutlines painted later will cover a small amount of the scumbled edges of the block.

- Masking will be required if the scumble technique is more random and free.

- Masking will take additional time. Try to paint without masking when possible to reduce painting time.

STEP 4
Bevel Shadow
and Highlight

Mix the **Shadow wash** and **Highlight wash** paint colors used for the beveled highlight and shadow.

- The consistency of the paint should be WATERY.
- Please test the paint. (See NOTES.)

Use a 1-1/2″ brush to paint the bevel.

- Don't cartoon the bevel. The brush and a straightedge will be sufficient.
- An angled bristle brush (sash brush) will work the best. Paint the highlight wash on the top and right of the block. Paint the shadow on the bottom and left of the block. A scenic fitch is also available with angled bristles. (See NOTES.)
- This brush stroke will have a point at either end. Achieving this stroke will take practice. Use the test flat to master the brush stroke before painting on the project flat. (See NOTES.)

Titles in **bold** indicate paint names found on the elevation.

Scale, 2 units wide × 3 units high.

NOTES

- Practice mixing and using shadow and highlight washes. It is important to master this skill. Highlight and shadow washes are used for every project. It will take practice.

- Please test all paints, especially shadow and highlight washes. Shadow wash will tend to dry with less intensity and highlight wash will tend to dry with more intensity. Or maybe not.

- Stir this paint on a regular basis. The pigment will settle more than paint of NORMAL consistency.

- A small flat (maybe 2′ × 3′) will work well as a test flat.

- An inexpensive, disposable foam brush is also a possible tool for painting the bevel.

Scale, 2 units wide × 3 units high.

STEP 5
Paint the Mortar

Use **Block scumble #3** for the mortar.

- The width of the brush is not critical when using the edge of a flat-ferrule brush.

- Paint with a scenic fitch or liner not more than 1/4″.

- A brush this size on the flat will not hold a great deal of paint. This will be a problem when painting longer lines.

- Experiment with a wider brush but use it on its side.

- These lines are straight, but the pressure can be variable.

- Use a straightedge. (See NOTES.)

- Paint the mortar between the blocks.

- Paint a small line on the outside of the blocks that share an edge with the textured wall.

Titles in **bold** indicate paint names found on the elevation.

NOTES

- Always use a straightedge for painting straight lines.

- "I can paint a straight line without a straightedge" or "It takes too long to paint and move a straightedge" or "It looks just fine without using a straightedge" are just a few of the excuses for not using a straightedge that are heard on a regular basis. All of these excuses are invalid!

- Mortar lines *must be straight and must line up vertically*. Masons are precise.

STEP 6
Cutlines

Add a small amount of additional water to the **Dark liner** paint color to paint the sharp dark cutlines.

- The dark sharp cutlines are used to clean up the scumbled block. Paint these lines on the left and bottom of each block.

- The dark sharp-edge lines are used to define the top of the block. Paint these lines on the left and bottom of each top plane of the block (the part of the block that is not beveled). This is a very small, subtle line. In fact, it might skip a bit.

- Use a straightedge.

Add a small amount of additional water to the **Light liner** paint color to paint the light sharp lines.

- The light sharp cutlines are used to clean up the scumbled block. Paint these lines on the right and top of each block.

- The light sharp-edge lines are used to define the top of block. Paint these lines on the top and right of the raised area of the block (the part of the block that is not beveled). This is a very small, subtle line. In fact, it might skip a bit.

- Use a straightedge.

Titles in **bold** indicate paint names found on the elevation.

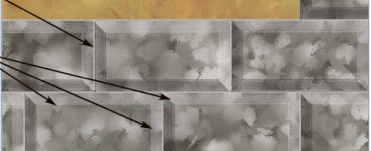

Scale, 2 units wide × 3 units high.

NOTES

- The purpose of cutlines is to duplicate small shadows and seams created by the joining of two or more objects.

- Don't use these lines to outline objects. Let highlight and shadow do that work.

- These lines add a bit of clarification when needed.

- These lines are very narrow—in some cases, too narrow to be seen. Use a brush with a very sharp edge. Don't press too hard. Paint with one stroke.

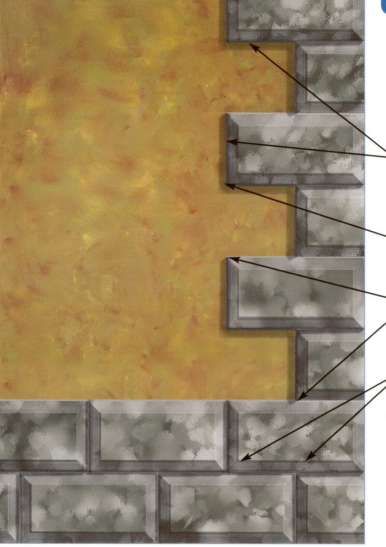

Scale, 2 units wide × 3 units high.

STEP 7
Shadow

Use the **Shadow wash** paint color for the block cast shadow.

- The consistency of the paint should be WATERY.
- Please test the paint. (See NOTES.)

Paint the cast shadows.

- The light is coming from the upper right. Paint the cast shadow on the bottom and left of the block. This is the cast shadow created because the block stands out from the wall.
- A small part of the shadow should overlap the edge of the block.
- Notice the angles on the top and bottom of the shadow.
- Paint a small shadow line on the left and on the bottom of the raised area of the block. This will help the eye perceive that this area is elevated above the bevel.

Titles in **bold** indicate paint names found on the elevation.

NOTES
- Highlight and shadow take considerable practice and are difficult to master, which is one big reason why this technique is a part of many projects.

STEP 8
Highlight

Use the **Highlight wash** paint color for the block highlight.

- The consistency of the paint should be WATERY.

- Please test the paint. (See NOTES.)

Paint the highlights.

- The light is coming from the upper right. Paint a small highlight on the top and on the right of the block.

- Paint a small highlight line on the right and on the top of the raised area of the block. This will help the eye perceive that this area is elevated above the bevel.

- These highlights are very subtle and should be very small.

- Don't paint a highlight in the middle of a block.

- This highlight is covered by the cast shadow from the adjoining block.

- How is that straightedge working out?

Titles in **bold** indicate paint names found on the elevation.

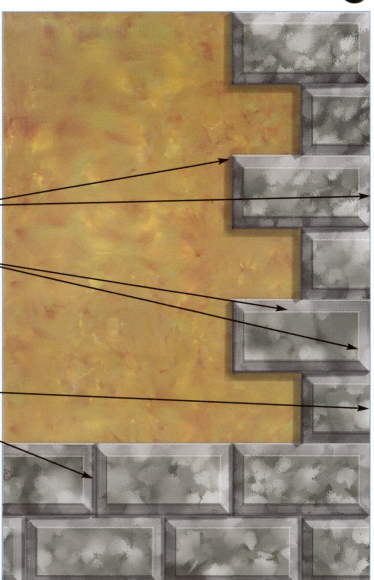

Scale, 2 units wide × 3 units high.

NOTES
- Mood and attitude affect the quality of scene painting. Plan ahead and try to avoid a last-minute rush.

- How long should it take to paint a project? Each painter is different, and there is no correct answer. Remember that most scenery is viewed from a distance. Don't spend time laboring over minute detail that an audience will not see.

- **P.S.** This wall and block look new and clean. Add weathering, stains, cracks, even moss growing between the cracks to give the wall an aged and distressed look.

Weathered Wood

WORK SURFACE

A 4′ × 6′ traditional or hard-covered flat.

TYPE OF PAINT

Rosco *Off Broadway* paint, Rosco *Iddings Deep Colors*, or a commercial latex substitute. See the COLOR SAMPLES page at the beginning of this book for brand and color suggestions.

TYPES OF CONSISTENCY

OUT OF THE CAN—Rosco suggests that the paint can be used right out of the can. This consistency might be thick. Add water to achieve a NORMAL consistency (see below).

NORMAL—Thick enough just to cover other projects in a single coat, assuming that the difference between the paint colors is not too great.

DILUTED—1 or 2 parts paint to 1 part water added to the NORMAL paint consistency.

WATERY—1 part paint to 5 to 10 parts water added to the NORMAL paint consistency. Rosco says: "Diluting with more than 2 parts water may reduce binder strength. Add Rosco *Clear Acrylic Glaze* to restore adhesion and flexibility."

PAINTING TECHNIQUES

BASE PAINT (paint technique)—The first paint color or colors used in a specific painting project, usually the predominant color.

CARTOON—A line drawing of a paint elevation used as a guide for a painting project.

DRY BRUSH (paint technique)—Dragging a brush loaded with paint across a dry surface (also called "combing").

SPATTER AND DRAG (paint technique)—Dragging spatter droplets of paint with a brush in order to produce a texture.

SHADOW WASH (paint technique)—A dark, transparent paint used to suggest a shadow cast from one object on another.

HIGHLIGHT WASH (paint technique)—a light, translucent paint used to represent the reflection of light or an area that receives the greatest amount of illumination.

Glossary

FLAT—A wooden frame secured with plywood fasteners and covered with material; a lighter alternative to a solid wall.

GRAINING (paint technique)—Creating a texture by dry brushing or combing to achieve a naturally formed pattern found in wood or marble.

KNOT HOLE—A hole in a board or tree trunk where a knot or branch has come out.

STRAIGHTEDGE—A straight length of wood with a handle that ensures the painting of a straight line.

TEST FLAT—A wooden frame secured with plywood fasteners and covered with material; built like a traditional flat but smaller.

Scale, 2 units wide × 3 units high.

TOOLS NEEDED
(See the Project pages for details.)

- **A collection of scene and housepainting brushes**
- **Chalk or charcoal for cartooning**
- **Tape measure**
- **Straightedge or lining stick**

Base Gray/burnt umber - light	**Window chipped** White/raw umber	**Shadow wash** Black/violet - 10% opacity	
Dry brush #1 Ultramarine blue	**Window trim** Chrome oxide green	**Highlight wash** Raw umber/white - 10% opacity	
Dry brush #2 Raw umber	**Detail light** Raw sienna		
Spatter and drag Black - 50% opacity	**Detail dark** Raw umber/black		

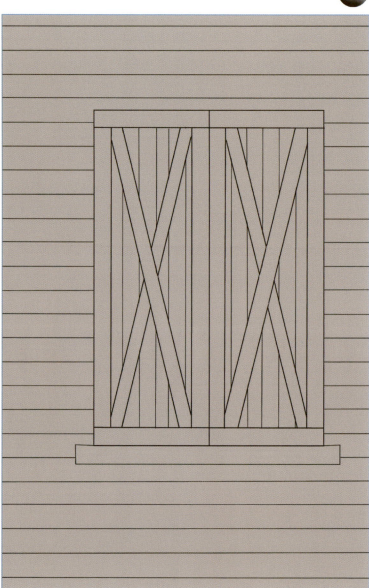

Scale, 2 units wide × 3 units high.

STEP 1
Base Paint and Cartoon the Flat

Base paint the flat with the **Base** color.

- If this flat is used for a scene painting class, the paint should be just thick enough to cover the previous painting project.

- If this is a new flat, the paint should be just thick enough to cover the flat.

- In either case, remember that a lot of additional paint will go on this flat. Use only enough paint to cover the flat.

- Let the flat dry completely.

Use chalk or charcoal to cartoon the planks.

- Please measure very carefully. Many projects are ruined because of mistakes made in measurement.

- Use a straightedge or chalk line to cartoon the straight lines. (See NOTES.)

Titles in **bold** indicate paint names found on the elevation.

IMPORTANT!

- It is important that painting techniques continue to the full extent of the prescribed area. The painting techniques of the back boards must go all the way to the window trim in this project. To achieve this:

  - Be very careful when painting.

  - Mask the window area with Kraft paper or other material before painting.

  - Paint through the window and frame and re-base the area after the wall is finished.

> **NOTES**
> - When cartooning a flat, use chalk or other light-color material on dark surfaces.
> - When cartooning a flat, use vine charcoal or other dark material on light surfaces.
> - Make sure that whatever is used can be removed or covered up when the cartoon lines are no longer needed.
> - Remember, some materials (such as a marker) will not always cover with paint. This might be a problem with the current project and might be a real problem when moving to the next project.

Things to Remember

5

Scale, 2 units wide × 3 units high.

5

STEP 2
Dry Brush and Spatter and Drag the Horizontal Wall Planks

Use a 3″ brush to paint **Dry brush #1**.

- The consistency of the paint should be the DILUTED type.

- Load the brush with a minimum of paint. Lightly press and move the brush over the flat. The **Base** should not be completely covered.

- Go as long as possible before lifting the brush or running out of paint. If the brush runs out of paint, lift it gradually so as to prevent a visible brush line.

- **Dry brush #1** is brighter than the other colors. Apply this color sparingly.

- Variation in the dry brush is desirable. Roll the brush when painting a plank or rotate the brush from side to side while keeping the bristles flat on the surface. Either method will achieve variation in the brush stroke.

Use a 3″ brush to paint **Dry brush #2**.

- The techniques previously explained also apply to this application.

Use a 3″ brush to paint **spatter and drag**.

- Use an old brush for spatter.

- Use a clean 3″ brush for dragging.

- Spatter a small area, attempting to work one plank at a time. Drag the clean brush immediately over the spatter.

Titles in **bold** indicate paint names found on the elevation.

NOTES

- A brand new and well cared for brush is not the best choice for the dry brush technique in this project.

- Please take care of paint brushes. Even with proper care, brushes will age and bristles will start to separate. Don't throw away these brushes, as they will work very well for this type of dry brush, spattering, and other painting techniques.

- Cut into the bristles of a new and inexpensive brush if an old brush is not available. This technique will ruin the brush for other applications.

- Inexpensive, disposable bristled brushes are great tools for painting this type of dry brush technique.

Things to Remember

Scale, 2 units wide × 3 units high.

STEP 3
Dry Brush the Window Planks

Use a 2″ brush to paint **Dry brush #2**.

- The techniques previously explained also apply to this application.

Use a 2″ brush to paint the **Window chipped** paint on the background of the window shutters.

- Old, weathered wood that at one time was painted with whitewash is the desired effect. The whitewash paint has weathered and flaked off through time. Achieving this effect will take experimentation and practice. Please try this technique on a test flat.

- A dry brush technique with NORMAL consistency paint might work well.

- Paint through the "X" trim pieces.

- Allow to dry.

- Re-base the "X" and the outside trim with the **Base**. (See NOTES.)

Titles in **bold** indicate paint names found on the elevation.

IMPORTANT!

- The finished effect should be the look of boards that once were whitewashed but are now weathered and peeling.

- Whitewash is a composition of lime and water or whiting (calcium carbonate ground into fine powder), size, and water. It is used for whitening structural surfaces.

NOTES

- Look at the picture. The left window shutter is an example of the flat after painting as instructed on this page. The right window shutter has the "X" and the outside trim re-based.

- Grain not going all the way to the ends and edges is a common problem with painting wood. (Also mentioned on the preceding page.) It is possible to mask the areas not to be painted. Painting the grain without going over the lines is another, although it is somewhat more difficult. Painting the affected areas again with **Base** is another solution. The painting situation will call for one of these techniques.

STEP 4
Dry Brush the
Window Frame

Use a 2″ brush to paint **Dry brush #2**.

- The consistency of the paint should be the DILUTED type.

- Load the brush with a minimum of paint. Lightly press and move the brush over the flat. The **Base** should not be completely covered.

- Go as long as possible before lifting the brush or running out of paint. If the brush runs out of paint, lift it gradually so as to prevent a visible brush line.

- Variation in the dry brush is desirable. Roll the brush when painting a plank or rotate the brush from side to side while keeping the bristles on the flat surface. Either method will achieve variation in the brush stroke.

Use a 2″ brush to paint **Window trim**.

- The techniques previously explained also apply to this application.

Use a 2″ brush to paint the **Window chipped** paint on the green trim of the window shutters.

- The techniques previously explained also apply to this application.

- Use a very small amount of the **Window chipped** paint color. The effect of the weathered whitewash on the green trim is less than that of the back of the shutters.

Titles in **bold** indicate paint names found on the elevation.

Scale, 2 units wide × 3 units high.

NOTES

- A wood grain "rocker" tool can be another method of painting wood grain.

- Plastic wood grain "rocker" tools are popular and can be purchased at most hardware and home improvement stores. A light base is applied and allowed to dry. A darker and more diluted paint is applied on top. A coarse grain is achieved by dragging the tool and simultaneously rocking the tool up and down. It is interesting, even fascinating, the way this tool works.

- The plastic wood graining tool does have its limitations. The results can lack a certain degree of sophistication without additional painting. Ideally, a smooth, hard surface is required. Sizes can limit effective application.

Things to Remember

STEP 5
Paint the Gaps Between the Planks

Prepare the **Detail dark** paint. Use a brush that will paint a 1/4″ line. Paint the horizontal lines between the planks.

- The consistency of the paint should be the DILUTED type.

- Don't use a straightedge to paint these lines. (See NOTES.)

- However, don't get too irregular with the lines. The wood has weathered and, as a result, the boards are worn. If the gaps are too big or too irregular, it will not look realistic.

Use a brush that will paint a slightly narrower line then the horizontal lines. Continue to use the **Detail dark** paint. Paint the vertical lines between the shutter boards.

- The consistency of the paint should be the DILUTED type.

- Don't use a straightedge to paint these lines. (See NOTES.)

- However, don't get too irregular with the lines. These gaps are smaller than the gaps between the wall planks.

Use the **Detail dark** to add few knotholes.

- They are not on the example; use discretion in their placement.

- Don't add too many, just a few for additional detail. (See NOTES.)

Titles in **bold** indicate paint names found on the elevation.

Scale, 2 units wide × 3 units high.

NOTES
- Always use a straightedge for painting straight lines.

- *This is important!* Don't use straightedge for this assignment.

- This is what lines look like without the aid of a straightedge, and the irregularity is welcome on this project. However, when straight lines are desired use a straightedge.

- Always keep in mind the direction of the light and how that light will effect the painting. In the case of holes, paint a highlight on the inside of the hole that faces the direction of the light (in this case, that will be the lower left inside).

Scale, 2 units wide × 3 units high.

STEP 6
Detail

Paint the hinges and handles.

- Measure, locate, and cartoon the hinges and handles.

- Use **Dry brush #2** and a small brush to base paint the hinges.

- Use **Detail light** and a small brush to paint the edges of the hinges that are toward the light. These lines must be straight.

- Use **Spatter and drag** and a small brush to paint the edges of the hinges that are away from the light. These lines must be straight.

- Use **Spatter and drag** to paint the three screws on each hinge. (See NOTES.)

- Use a small amount of **Detail light** as a highlight for the screw. Use a small amount of **Spatter and drag** as a shadow for the screw. This is very quick and not very precise.

Use **Spatter and drag** to paint a few cutlines.

- These lines are on the green window frame.

- These cutlines represent the small lines created by the joining of the wood frame.

- These are small, fine lines—not too big.

Titles in **bold** indicate paint names found on the elevation.

NOTES

- Use a small brush or a finger to base the screws. Don't work hard to get these perfect.

- Always keep in mind the direction of the light and how that light will affect the painting.

- In the case of holes, paint a highlight on the inside of the hole that faces the direction of the light (in this case, that will be the lower left inside).

STEP 7
Shadow

Mix the **Shadow wash** at 10% opacity.

- Consider adding additional binder.
- Please test. (See NOTES.)

Shadow the horizontal boards.

- Use the **Shadow wash** to paint the lower edge of the horizontal boards and the left side of the vertical boards. This will read as thickness.
- This shadow should be about 1/2″.

Painting the cast shadows.

- Use the **Shadow wash** and a 1″ brush to paint under the lower edge of the top window frame, on the right inside of the side window frame, on each "X," and around the handles and hinges.
- Use the **Shadow wash** and a 1-1/2″ brush to paint under the lower edge of the window sill and on the left side of the window frame. (See NOTES.)

Paint the gap around the shutters.

- Use **Spatter and drag** to paint a separation between the shutters.
- Use **Spatter and drag** to paint a separation at the bottom of the shutters.

Titles in **bold** indicate paint names found on the elevation.

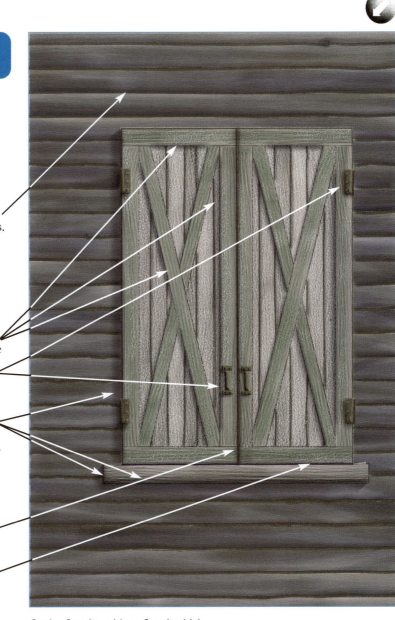

Scale, 2 units wide × 3 units high.

NOTES

- Practice mixing and using washes. This technique *must* be mastered. Washes are used in almost every project. It will take practice.

- Please test all paints, especially washes. Darker washes will tend to dry with less intensity and lighter washes will tend to dry with more intensity (but it is very unpredictable).

- A small flat (maybe 2′ × 3′) will work well as a test flat.

- Stir this paint a lot. It will settle more than paint of NORMAL or DILUTED consistency.

- When painting cast shadows, keep the bottom edge of the brush parallel with the light direction. This will automatically line up the shadows with the direction of the light.

Scale, 2 units wide × 3 units high.

STEP 8
Highlight

Mix the **Highlight wash** at 10% opacity.

- Consider adding additional binder.
- Please test. (See NOTES.)

Paint the highlight on the window shutters. Use the **Highlight wash** and the edge of a brush to paint:

- On the top and right edge of the window frame.
- On the edges of each "X."
- On the left and bottom inside of the window frame.
- Remember that these boards are worn and do not have sharp edges to reflect sharp highlights. The highlights on the boards are not large and are not consistent.

Paint the highlight on the boards. Use the **Highlight wash** to paint the top edge of the horizontal.

- Remember that these boards are worn and do not have sharp edges to reflect sharp highlights. The highlights on the boards are not large and are not consistent.

Titles in **bold** indicate paint names found on the elevation.

NOTES

- Please test all paints, especially washes. Darker washes will tend to dry with less intensity and lighter washes will tend to dry with more intensity (but it is very unpredictable).

- **P.S.** Consider painting additional dirt and distressing:

  - More stains could be added to the boards, especially under the window.

  - The wall boards could be in extreme dilapidation; planks could be missing, and some might hang on angles.

  - Organic material might be found at the bottom of the wall as it meets the ground.

Things to Remember _____

5

Stylized Landscape

WORK SURFACE

A 4′ × 6′ traditional or hard-covered flat.

TYPE OF PAINT

Rosco *Off Broadway* paint, Rosco *Iddings Deep Colors*, or a commercial latex substitute. See the COLOR SAMPLES page at the beginning of this book for brand and color suggestions.

TYPES OF CONSISTENCY

OUT OF THE CAN—Rosco suggests that the paint can be used right out of the can. This consistency might be thick. Add water to achieve a NORMAL consistency (see below).

NORMAL—Thick enough just to cover other projects in a single coat, assuming that the difference between the paint colors is not too great.

DILUTED—1 or 2 parts paint to 1 part water added to the NORMAL paint consistency.

WATERY—1 part paint to 5 to 10 parts water added to the NORMAL paint consistency. Rosco says: "Diluting with more than 2 parts water may reduce binder strength. Add Rosco *Clear Acrylic Glaze* to restore adhesion and flexibility."

PAINTING TECHNIQUES

SCUMBLE (paint technique)—Blending two or more random patches of color; the size of the patches and the amount of blend will vary depending on the project.

CARTOON—A line drawing of a paint elevation used as a guide for a painting project.

SHADOW WASH (paint technique)—A dark, transparent paint used to suggest a shadow cast from one object on another.

HIGHLIGHT WASH (paint technique)—A light, translucent paint used to represent the reflection of light or an area that receives the greatest amount of illumination.

Glossary

GRID—A method of transferring a cartoon; a collection of lines and squares in a scale on a paint elevation and in full scale on a drop or flat.

HATCHING—To draw or paint with fine, closely spaced lines, especially to give an effect of shading.

FLOGGER—A short piece of wood about 2″ long with strips of muslin attached to the end. [′ is feet, ″ is inches.] It is used to remove cartoon lines, dust, and dirt from a painting surface by whipping the surface.

WASH—The thinning of paint to achieve transparency.

FOLIAGE—A representation of leaves, flowers, and branches for architectural ornamentation.

CHARCOAL (VINE)—A stick of fine charred softwood used in drawing.

CHALK—A stick of soft white or buff limestone composed chiefly of the shells of foraminifers.

TRANSLUCENT—Transmitting and diffusing light so objects beyond cannot be seen clearly; light may pass through, but the material is not transparent.

Scale, 2 units wide × 3 units high.

TOOLS NEEDED
(See the Project pages for details.)

- **A collection of scene and housepainting brushes**
- **Chalk or charcoal for cartooning**
- **Tape measure**
- **Straightedge or lining stick**
- **Flogger**
- **Colored nylon string and "T" pins**

Scumble #1 — Yellow ochre	**Sun wash #1** — Lemon yellow - 10% opacity	**Dark rock wash** — Sky blue/dark gray - 10% opacity
Scumble #2 — Raw sienna	**Sun wash #2** — Yellow ochre - 10% opacity	**Light rock wash** — Sky blue/light gray - 10% opacity
Scumble #3 — Lemon yellow	**Tree trunk wash** — Burnt sienna - 10% opacity	**Shadow foliage wash** — Purple - 10% opacity
Hatch lines — Raw umber	**Light foliage wash** — Emerald green - 10% opacity	

Scale, 2 units wide × 3 units high.

STEP 1
Scumble the Background

Use **Scumble #1**, **Scumble #2,** and **Scumble #3** for the scumble base. (See NOTES.)

- Add a little more water to the NORMAL consistency paint. This will help the blending process.

Use a 2″ or 3″ brush to paint patches of all three scumble colors.

- Work a quarter of the flat at a time.
- The patches of color can touch each other but should not blend at this time.
- Either use three brushes or clean the brush out a bit after applying each color.
- Before the paint dries, use a clean brush to blend the colors. Use an omnidirectional brush stroke when blending the colors together.
- Don't overwork the blending. The goal is to have a number of colors as a result of the blending. There should be places where the three colors are not blended at all.
- The colors are close in contrast and the blending and brush strokes are small in this project. (See NOTES.)

Titles in **bold** indicate paint names found on the elevation.

NOTES
- In terms of time, scumble should take only a little longer than base painting. Scumble shouldn't be a quick technique, but it adds more interest than one color of base paint.

- Two major factors affect the look of scumble: One is the number and contrast of the paint colors, and the second is the sizes of the brushes used for the technique.

STEP 2
Cartoon with a Grid

Using a grid.

- A grid on the flat will provide a frame of reference as a method for cartooning the image.
- The paint example to the right is divided into 1/2-unit squares.
- The flat to paint is also divided into 1/2-unit squares.
- Transfer the visual information in each square of the elevation to each square on the flat.
- Pay particular attention to where cartoon lines cross the lines of the grid squares.

Draw the grid.

- Measure and mark all sides of the flat into 1/2-unit marks.
- Use a snap line to draw the grid. (See NOTES.)

Alternative method for drawing a grid.

- Measure and mark all sides of the flat into 1/2-unit marks.
- Stick "T" pins in the floor just off the flat if painting down. Stick "T" pins in the side of the flat if painting up.
- Weave a colored nylon string around the pins to create the same grid without chalking the flat.

Titles in **bold** indicate paint names found on the elevation.

Scale, 2 units wide × 3 units high.

The grid on the elevation is drawn in blue to help see it clearly. It should be black charcoal, white chalk, or colored string.

NOTES

- A grid is a useful method for cartooning when the shapes drawn are natural and nonarchitectural.

- A grid the size of this project is small and too confusing under most circumstances. A bigger grid should be constructed on larger projects, such as a full drop.

- The blue or red chalk found in most shop snap lines will be difficult to remove from the flat. A new snap line filled with charcoal power will be a great addition to scene painting equipment.

- Consider labeling the grid lines when working with a large project.

Things to Remember

STEP 3
Cartoon the Flat

Use chalk or vine charcoal to cartoon the landscape. (See NOTES.)

- Please measure very carefully. Take time to avoid mistakes.

- Many projects are less than successful because of mistakes made in measurement.

- Consider cartooning shapes as well as using the grid. This might help to make the process less confusing.

- Try to work fast and don't be too detailed. This project can be very time consuming.

Remove the grid using a flogger.

- The handle of a flogger is made from a short piece of wood about 2′ long.

- Attach strips of muslin to the end of the handle. These strips are about 18″ long.

- Use the flogger to beat the flat and remove the charcoal grid.

Titles in **bold** indicate paint names found on the elevation.

Scale, 2 units wide × 3 units high.

IMPORTANT!
- Wait to remove the grid until after the cartoon lines are painted. They might be helpful when painting the hatching.

NOTES

- When cartooning a flat, use chalk or other light-color material on dark surfaces.

- When cartooning a flat, use vine charcoal or other dark material on light surfaces.

- Make sure that whatever is used can be removed or covered up when cartoon lines are no longer needed.

- Remember, some materials (such as marker) will not always cover with paint. This might be a problem with the current project and might be a real problem when moving to the next project.

- A flogger can also be used to remove dust and dirt from drops and flats.

Things to Remember

STEP 4
Paint Hatch Lines

Use the **Hatch lines** color to paint the lines in the sky.

- Lightly chalk the cloud area and the halo around the sun.

- Use a brush designed to paint sharp, straight lines. A good-quality commercial paint brush will work well.

- Start painting at the bottom or at the top. Use a straightedge to paint these lines. (See NOTES.)

- Be careful not to cross the cloud or sun lines.

- Use light pressure and a loose touch when painting the hatch lines.

Use the **Hatch lines** color to paint the next set of lines.

- Paint small cross-hatch lines in the shadow of the clouds—no need for a straightedge.

- Consider chalking in the area before painting.

- Repeat this procedure when painting the island, water, and shadow side of the rocks.

Titles in **bold** indicate paint names found on the elevation.

Scale, 2 units wide × 3 units high.

IMPORTANT!
- Make sure to use a brush capable of painting sharp, thin lines. Thick and blotchy lines will spoil the look of this project.

NOTES

- To measure or not to measure, that is the question. Accurately measuring and placing these lines on the flat will produce a wonderful final product. But at what price? All that measuring will slow the painting process way down and probably drive the painter crazy.

- Use the cartooned shapes and the grid (if it can be seen) to line up the hatch lines.

- Measure periodically to make sure the lines are parallel to the top and bottom of the flat. If not, correct gradually.

- Above all, the look and feel of this project is more important than complete accuracy!

Things to Remember

STEP 5
Paint Hatch Lines

- Use the **Hatch lines** color to paint the lines that will be foliage.

- Use a brush that holds a lot of paint but is capable of painting a smaller width line. It is likely that this brush will be different from the brush used for the sky lines on the previous page.

- Use a light touch.

- Work to achieve the look and feeling of the elevation. Don't try to duplicate it exactly.

- The line width will vary. Not all lines are the same width.

- Keep in mind the direction of the light. More lines suggest less light.

Use the **Hatch lines** color to paint the cross-hatching on the shadow side of the tree trunks.

- Consider using the brush used for the sky hatching.

- Consider chalking in the area before painting.

- Use light pressure and a loose touch when painting the hatch lines.

Titles in **bold** indicate paint names found on the elevation.

Scale, 2 units wide × 3 units high.

NOTES
- A hatching style of painting has a high degree of success. Nonprofessional painters can achieve excellent results painting in this style.

- It is important not to overpaint or overanalyze this style of painting. It is very possible to overwork this project as well as this style of painting.

- Have fun and work quickly.

Scale, 2 units wide × 3 units high.

STEP 6
Paint Colored Wash

Prepare the **Sky wash** used to paint the sky area. (See NOTES.)

- Vary the concentration of the **Sky wash**. Some areas of the sky contain little paint.

- It probably took longer to mix and test this paint then it will to paint this area. This is a very quick application of paint.

- *Do not overwork.* Excessive brush strokes will begin to pick up the paint used for the scumble and for hatching.

Prepare the **Tree trunk wash** used to paint the tree trunks. (See NOTES.)

- The techniques previously explained also apply to this application.

- The **Tree trunk wash** is more concentrated on the left side (shadow side) of the tree trunks.

Prepare **Sun wash #1** and **Sun wash #2** for painting the sun. (See NOTES.)

- The techniques previously explained also apply to this application.

- This is a very small amount of paint. One paint brush dipped in the appropriate color can be mixed in or on most anything. Don't waste paint or time.

Titles in **bold** indicate paint names found on the elevation.

NOTES

- All the colored washes in this project are listed at 10% opacity. As with all paint consistencies, this is a starting point. Varied factors contribute to the success of the final painting. All these factors cannot be controlled in this book; therefore, it is very important to test these washes on a test flat that has a scumbled base and different hatch and cross-hatch lines.

STEP 7
Paint Colored Wash

Prepare the paint for the foliage. (See NOTES.)

- Apply the **Shadow foliage wash** in the shadow area of the foliage.

- Vary the concentration of the **Shadow foliage wash**.

- *Do not overwork.* Excessive brush strokes will begin to pick up the paint used for the scumble and for hatching.

- Repeat this process using the **Light foliage wash** and the **Dark foliage wash**.

Prepare the paint for the rocks. (See NOTES.)

- Apply the **Dark rock wash** in the shadow area of the rock.

- Apply the **Light rock wash** on the opposite side (the side toward the light) of the rock.

- Paint the water.

- Use the **Light foliage wash** and the **Sky wash** to paint the water area. Maybe sneak in a bit of the **Shadow foliage wash**.

- *Do not overwork.* Excessive brush strokes will begin to pick up the paint used for the scumble and for hatching.

Titles in **bold** indicate paint names found on the elevation.

Scale, 2 units wide × 3 units high.

NOTES
- This is a repeat from the previous page. It is important!

- All the colored washes in this project are listed at 10% opacity. As with all paint consistencies, this is a starting point. Varied factors contribute to the success of the final painting. All these factors cannot be controlled in this book. Therefore, it is very important to test these washes on a test flat that has a scumbled base and different hatch and cross-hatch lines.

Bookshelf

WORK SURFACE

A 4′ × 6′ traditional or hard-covered flat.

TYPE OF PAINT

Rosco *Off Broadway* paint, Rosco *Iddings Deep Colors*, or a commercial latex substitute. See the COLOR SAMPLES page at the beginning of this book for brand and color suggestions.

TYPES OF CONSISTENCY

OUT OF THE CAN—Rosco suggests that the paint can be used right out of the can. This consistency might be thick. Add water to achieve a NORMAL consistency (see below).

NORMAL—Thick enough just to cover other projects in a single coat, assuming that the difference between the paint colors is not too great.

DILUTED—1 or 2 parts paint to 1 part water added to the NORMAL paint consistency.

WATERY—1 part paint to 5 to 10 parts water added to the NORMAL paint consistency. Rosco says: "Diluting with more than 2 parts water may reduce binder strength. Add Rosco *Clear Acrylic Glaze* to restore adhesion and flexibility."

PAINTING TECHNIQUES

BASE PAINT (paint technique)—The first paint color or colors used in a specific painting project; usually the predominant color.

CARTOON—A line drawing of a paint elevation used as a guide for a painting project.

DRY BRUSH (paint technique)—Dragging a brush loaded with paint across a dry surface (also called "combing").

CUTLINE (paint technique)—Small detail lines that help to differentiate edges and planes.

SHADOW WASH (paint technique)—A dark, transparent paint used to suggest a shadow cast from one object on another.

HIGHLIGHT WASH (paint technique)—A light, translucent paint used to represent the reflection of light or an area that receives the greatest amount of illumination.

Glossary

FLAT—A wooden frame secured with plywood fasteners and covered with material; a lighter alternative to a solid wall.

MARKER—A permanent-ink, felt-tipped pen used for setting cartoon lines; they are available in many tip widths and colors.

SHADOW WASH (paint technique)—A dark, transparent paint used to suggest a shadow cast from one object on another.

STRAIGHTEDGE—A straight length of wood with a handle that ensures the painting of a straight line.

TEST FLAT—A wooden frame secured with plywood fasteners and covered with material; built like a traditional flat but smaller.

CHARCOAL (VINE)—A stick of fine charred softwood used in drawing.

CHALK—A stick of soft white or buff limestone composed chiefly of the shells of foraminifers.

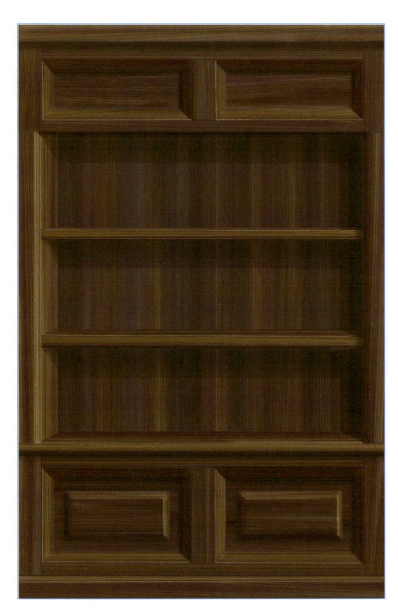

Scale, 2 units wide × 3 units high.

TOOLS NEEDED
(See the Project pages for details.)

- **A collection of scene and housepainting brushes**
- **Chalk or charcoal for cartooning**
- **Tape measure**
- **Straightedge or lining stick**

Wood base Burnt umber	**Dark panel wash** Umber/black - 20% opacity	**Light cut line** Raw sienna - medium
Wood grain #1 Burnt sienna	**Light panel wash** Raw sienna - 20% opacity	**Shadow wash** Black - 10% opacity
Wood grain #2 Raw sienna	**Dark cut line** Burnt sienna - dark	**Highlight wash** Raw sienna light - 10% opacity

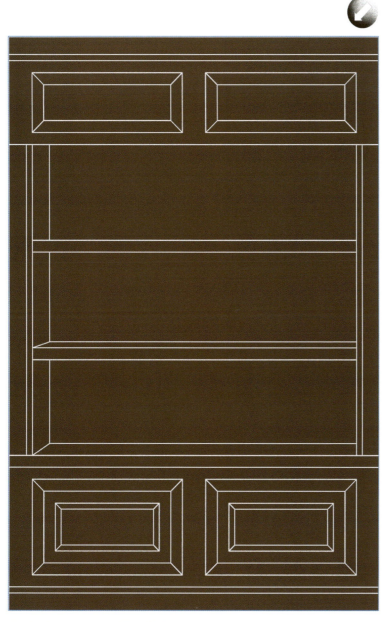

Scale, 2 units wide × 3 units high.

STEP 1
Base Paint and
Cartoon the Flat

Base paint the flat with the **Wood base**.

* If this flat has been used, the paint should be just thick enough to cover the previous painting project.

* Dip the brush in a small amount of paint. Remember to use the tips of the brush.

* Use an omnidirectional brush stroke when base painting.

* Avoid holidays.

Use chalk or charcoal to cartoon the flat. (See NOTES.)

* Please measure very carefully. Many projects are ruined because of mistakes made in measurement.

* There are many ways to approach cartooning a flat. The next page illustrates one method for cartooning this project.

Titles in **bold** indicate paint names found on the elevation.

IMPORTANT!

* White lines are easier to see in the example. They were used on this page and the next page to improve measuring and cartooning. Later examples are cartooned in black. Chalk or charcoal will work equally well. As the painter of the project, decide which is appropriate.

NOTES

- When cartooning a flat, use chalk or other light-color material on dark surfaces and use vine charcoal or other dark material on light surfaces.

- Make sure that whatever is used can be removed or covered up with paint when the guides are no longer required.

- Some materials (such as marker) will not always cover with paint. This might be a problem with a current project and might be a real problem with the next project.

Things to Remember

HOW TO LAY OUT THIS PROJECT

New lines in each phase are yellow.

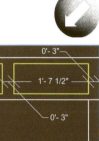

Phase one. Top and sides of the shelf opening.

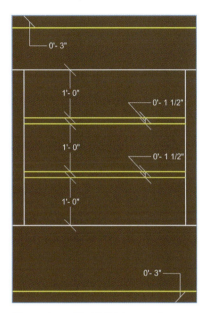

Phase two. Shelf thickness, top trim, and bottom baseboard.

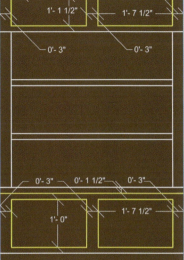

Phase three. Shelf opening bottom trim and outside of the panels.

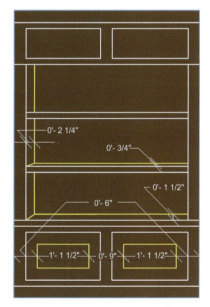

Phase four. Inside of the shelf opening and the surface of the shelves.

Phase five. Trim and panel bevel. (Note: Use a 1-1/2″ brush or a 3/4″ brush and the lines of the panel as an alternative to cartooning the bevel.)

Phase six. Finished cartoon.

STEP 2
Dry Brush the Back of the Bookshelf

Use a 4″ brush to paint **Wood grain #1**.

- The consistency of the paint should have a little more water than NORMAL.

- Load the brush with a minimum of paint. Lightly press and move the brush vertically over the flat. The **Wood base** should not be completely covered.

- Variation in the dry brush is desirable. Roll the brush when painting a plank or rotate the brush from side to side while keeping the bristles flat on the surface. Either method will achieve variation in the brush stroke.

Clean and use the same brush to paint **Wood grain #2**.

- The techniques previously explained also apply to this application.

Clean and use the same brush to paint the **Dark panel wash** over the same area.

- This paint has more water than the dry brush paint.

- Vary the amount of wash and the areas painted.

Titles in **bold** indicate paint names found on the elevation.

Scale, 2 units wide × 3 units high.

IMPORTANT!
- The example on this page represents the finished product. Either dry brush the area and re-base the shelves or mask the area before dry brushing.

> **IMPORTANT!**
>
> • It is vital that the wood grain painting goes all the way to the edge of the area. Consider painting over the chalk edge and then repainting the base.
>
> • A brand new and well cared for brush is not the best choice for the dry brush technique in this project.
>
> • Please take care of paint brushes. Even with proper care, brushes will age and bristles will begin to separate. Don't throw away these brushes. They will work very well for this type of dry brush, spattering, and other painting techniques.
>
> • Cut into the bristles of a new and inexpensive brush if an old brush is not available. This technique will ruin the brush for other applications.

Things to Remember

STEP 3
Dry Brush the Panels and Trim

Use a 3″ or 4″ brush to paint **Wood grain #1**.

- The consistency of the paint should have a little more water than NORMAL.

- Load the brush with a minimum of paint. Lightly press and move the brush vertically over the flat. The **Wood base** should not completely cover.

- Variation in the dry brush is desirable. Roll the brush when painting a plank or rotate the brush from side to side while keeping the bristles flat on the surface. Either method will achieve variation in the brush stroke.

Clean and use the same brush to paint **Wood grain #2**.

- The techniques previously explained also apply to this application.

Clean and use the same brush to paint the **Dark panel wash** over the same area.

- This paint has more water than the dry brush paint.

- Vary the amount of wash and the areas painted.

Titles in **bold** indicate paint names found on the elevation.

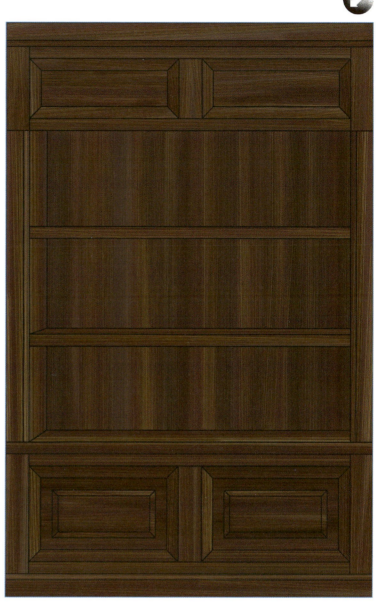

Scale, 2 units wide × 3 units high.

IMPORTANT!
- It is vital that the wood grain painting goes all the way to the edge of the area. Previously painted edges will be covered if painted in the proper order. (See NOTES.)

NOTES

- Paint the items that appear to be in the back and work forward. The paint applied will cover the edges from previous painting. Here is the order of painting for the bottom panel; use this approach for the remainder of the flat:

1. Back panel
2. Bevels from panels
3. Center toggle
4. Bottom and top rails
5. Side stiles
6. Bottom base trim

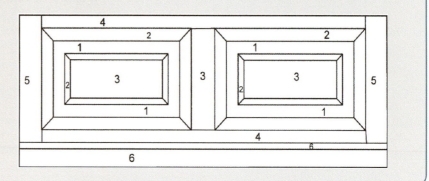

Things to Remember

STEP 4
Panel Wash

Give the trim and panels the illusion of dimension with washes.

- Paint the "1" areas with **Dark panel wash**.
- Paint the "2" areas with **Light panel wash**.

Look at the example to the right. Use the **Light panel wash** to paint:

- The left edge of the shelf side
- The top of the shelf front

Use the **Dark panel wash** to paint:

- The top and right edge of the shelf side
- The bottom of the shelf front

Titles in **bold** indicate paint names found on the elevation.

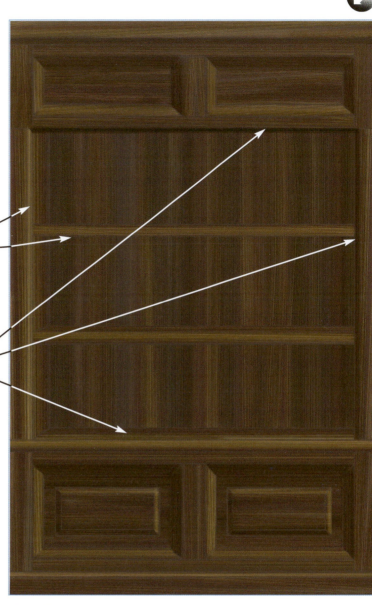

Scale, 2 units wide × 3 units high.

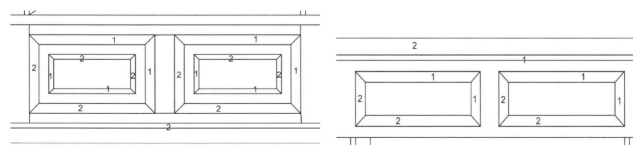

Top panels.

Bottom panels.

> **NOTES**
> - Not painting all the way to the edges of a designated paint area is a common problem for beginning painters. Techniques should go to the extents of the designated painting area.
> - Make sure that all techniques are complete. Spatter, dry brush, splatter, etc. all must go to the edges of the flat or area.
> - Failure to do so will negatively affect the look of the finished painting.
> - Use a drop cloth so paint should not end up on surrounding areas.

Things to Remember

STEP 5
Cutlines

Look at the example. Use the **Dark cutline** to paint:

- Beneath the top trim piece
- The top, bottom, and common edge of the bevels
- The bottom edge of the shelves
- The places where the shelf meets the sides of the bookshelf
- The top, bottom, and common edge of the bevels on the raised panels (the lower and left side of the raised panel); the technique is the same as that for the top panels

Look at the example. Use the **Light cutline** to paint:

- The top edge of the top trim piece
- The top, bottom, and common edge of the bevels (the lower and left side of the recessed panel); the same technique is the same as that for the bottom panels
- The top edge of the shelves
- The top, bottom, and common edge of the bevels on the raised panels (the upper and right side of the raised panel)

Titles in **bold** indicate paint names found on the elevation.

Scale, 2 units wide × 3 units high.

IMPORTANT!

- The purpose of cutlines is to duplicate the look of small shadows and seams created by the joining together of two or more objects.

- Don't use these lines to outline objects. Let highlight and shadow do that work.

- Cutlines add a bit of clarification when needed.

- Cutlines are very narrow—in some cases, they are too narrow to see. Use a brush with a very sharp edge, and don't press too hard. One pass is sufficient. It is acceptable, even desirable, for the paint to skip.

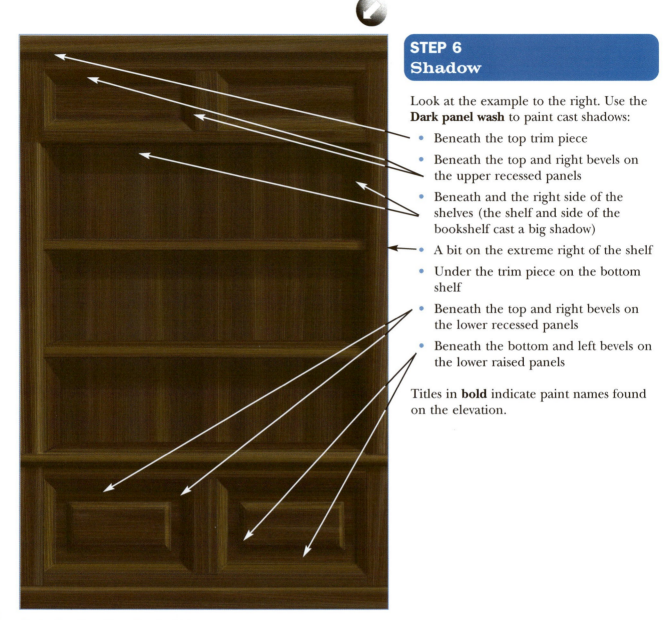

Scale, 2 units wide × 3 units high.

STEP 6
Shadow

Look at the example to the right. Use the **Dark panel wash** to paint cast shadows:

- Beneath the top trim piece
- Beneath the top and right bevels on the upper recessed panels
- Beneath and the right side of the shelves (the shelf and side of the bookshelf cast a big shadow)
- A bit on the extreme right of the shelf
- Under the trim piece on the bottom shelf
- Beneath the top and right bevels on the lower recessed panels
- Beneath the bottom and left bevels on the lower raised panels

Titles in **bold** indicate paint names found on the elevation.

NOTES

- Practice mixing and using washes. This technique *must* be mastered. Washes are used in almost every project. It will take practice.

- Please test all paints, especially washes. Darker washes will tend to dry with less intensity and lighter washes will tend to dry with more intensity (but it is very unpredictable).

- A small flat (maybe 2′ × 3′) will work well as a test flat.

- Stir this paint a lot. Pigment will settle more than paint of NORMAL or DILUTED consistency.

STEP 7
Highlight

Look at the example to the right. Use the **Highlight wash** to paint:

- The edge of the top trim piece
- The bottom and left bevels on the upper recessed panels
- The top of the front of the shelf
- The left side of the shelf reveal
- The edge of the left trim piece
- The top of the trim piece on the bottom shelf
- The top and right bevels on the lower raised panels
- The bottom and left bevels on the lower recessed panels
- The top beveled edge on the baseboard trim

Titles in **bold** indicate paint names found on the elevation.

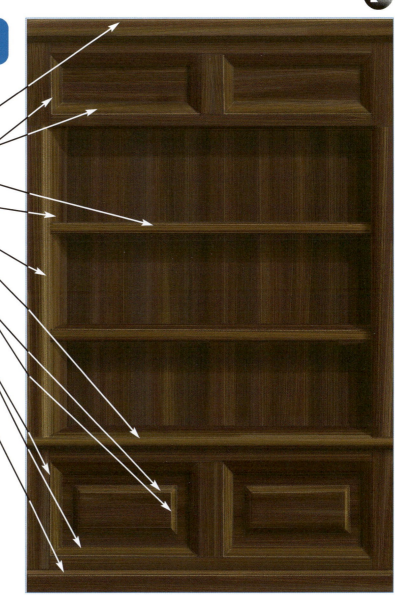

Scale, 2 units wide × 3 units high.

NOTES

- Please test all paints, especially washes. Darker washes will tend to dry with less intensity and lighter washes will tend to dry with more intensity (but it is very unpredictable).

- **P.S.** Consider adding items to the shelf:

  - Books would be the first choice (see the next project, a continuation of this project).

  - Trophies, decorative boxes, statuary, and small pictures are all possibilities.

  - Organic material (plants of all sorts) might also be found on the shelves.

  - It is possible to make such additions very involved and complicated.

Books Added to Bookshelf

WORK SURFACE

A 4′ × 6′ traditional or hard-covered flat.

TYPE OF PAINT

Rosco *Off Broadway* paint, Rosco *Iddings Deep Colors*, or a commercial latex substitute. See the COLOR SAMPLES page at the beginning of this book for brand and color suggestions.

TYPES OF CONSISTENCY

OUT OF THE CAN—Rosco suggests that the paint can be used right out of the can. This consistency might be thick. Add water to achieve a NORMAL consistency (see below).

NORMAL—Thick enough just to cover other projects in a single coat, assuming that the difference between the paint colors is not too great.

DILUTED—1 or 2 parts paint to 1 part water added to the NORMAL paint consistency.

WATERY—1 part paint to 5 to 10 parts water added to the NORMAL paint consistency. Rosco says: "Diluting with more than 2 parts water may reduce binder strength. Add Rosco *Clear Acrylic Glaze* to restore adhesion and flexibility."

PAINTING TECHNIQUES

CARTOON—A line drawing of a paint elevation used as a guide for a painting project.

WET BLEND (paint technique)—Combining two or more colors on a painting surface while still wet.

HIGHLIGHT WASH (paint technique)—A light, translucent paint used to represent the reflection of light or an area that receives the greatest amount of illumination.

SHADOW WASH (paint technique)—A dark, transparent paint used to suggest a shadow cast from one object on another.

Glossary

BLEND—To combine so that the line of demarcation cannot be distinguished.

BRUSH—Device composed of bristles typically set into a handle and used especially for sweeping, smoothing, scrubbing, or painting.

CHALK—A stick of soft white or buff limestone composed chiefly of the shells of foraminifers.

CHARCOAL (VINE)—A stick of fine charred softwood used in drawing.

MARKER—A permanent-ink, felt-tipped pen used for setting cartoon lines; they are available in many tip widths and colors.

OPAQUE—Paint that cannot be seen through and hides what is underneath.

ROLLED HIGHLIGHT (paint technique)—A translucent highlight with one hard edge and one blended edge to suggest a curved or rounded surface.

ROLLED SHADOW (paint technique)—A translucent shadow with one hard edge and one blended edge to suggest a curved or rounded surface.

STRAIGHTEDGE—A straight length of wood with a handle that ensures the painting of a straight line.

TRANSLUCENT—Transmitting and diffusing light so objects beyond cannot be seen clearly; light may pass through, but the material is not transparent.

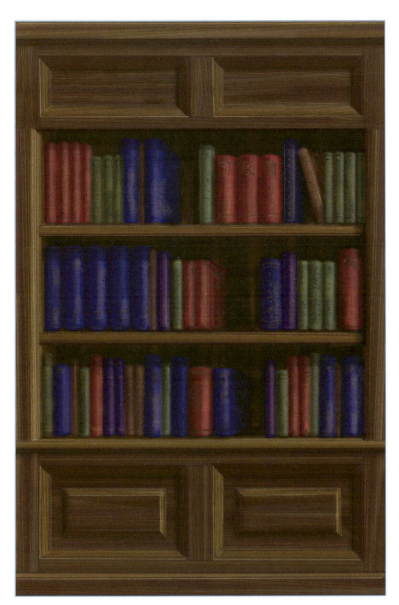

Scale, 2 units wide × 3 units high.

LIGHT DIRECTION

TOOLS NEEDED
(See the Project pages for details.)

- A collection of scene and housepainting brushes

- Chalk or charcoal for cartooning

- Tape measure

- Straightedge or lining stick

 Book base #1
Ultramarine blue

 Book base #2
Deep red

 Book base #3
Chrome oxide green

 Book base #4
Purple

 **Book base #5**
Burnt sienna

Hightlight wash
Gray - light - 10% opacity

Shadow wash
Black - 10% opacity

 Book detail #1
Yellow ochre

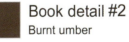 **Book detail #2**
Burnt umber

 Book detail #3
Black

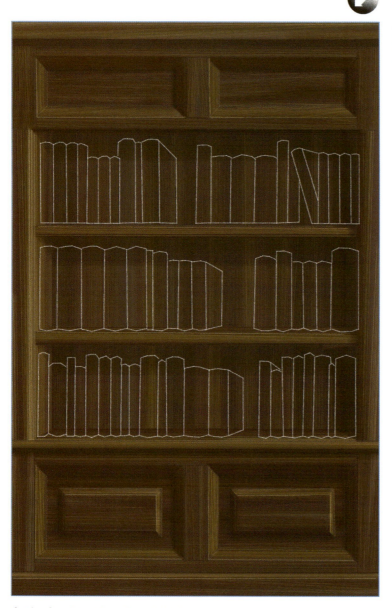

Scale, 2 units wide × 3 units high.

STEP 1
Cartoon the Flat

Use chalk or charcoal to cartoon the books.

- Please measure very carefully. Many projects are ruined because of mistakes made in measurement.

- There is an alternative method to complete cartooning of the books. Draw small marks at the bottom of each shelf that indicate the thickness of the book. A small mark can be placed at the top of the book. Use an appropriate size brush to paint the book base color.

- This saves time because not all of the books are cartooned, but it will be more difficult to keep the book color, width, and height correct.

Titles in **bold** indicate paint names found on the elevation.

NOTES

- When cartooning a flat, use chalk or other light-color material on dark surfaces.

- When cartooning a flat, use vine charcoal or other dark material on light surfaces.

- Make sure that whatever is used can be removed or covered up when the cartoon lines are no longer needed.

- Remember, some materials (such as marker) will not always cover with paint. This might be a problem with the current project and might be a real problem when painting the next project.

STEP 2
Base and Wet Blend the Books

Use **Book base #1** to paint the blue books.

- Use a brush the width of the book and a smaller straightedge for the books. A 6′ straightedge is difficult to handle for small painting.

- Paint one-third of the left side of each book with **Shadow wash** and one-third of the right side of the book with **Highlight wash** while the base paint is still wet.

- Have a clean brush handy to blend the book surface. The base brush used to paint the books will work for this purpose but should be cleaned regularly.

- Don't work too hard to get a perfect blend from the three paints. The effect will be diminished if the blend is overworked.

Use **Book base #2**, **Book base #3**, **Book base #4**, and **Book base #5** to base and blend the remainder of the books.

- Paint the rest of the books, one color at a time.

- Brushes will not require cleaning as often.

- It will also give like color books time to dry to avoid unwanted blending.

- Use the same procedure as the blue books.

Titles in **bold** indicate paint names found on the elevation.

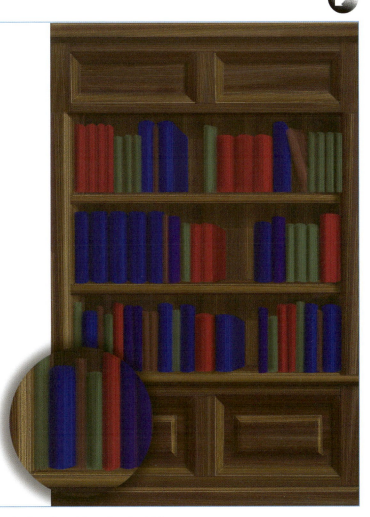

Scale, 2 units wide × 3 units high.

NOTES

- Always use a straightedge for painting straight lines.

- It is tempting not to use a straightedge when painting small areas. Speed and quality will improve with the use of a straightedge.

- Mood and attitude affect the quality of scene painting. Plan ahead and try to avoid a last-minute rush.

- How long should it take to paint a project? Each painter is different and there is no correct answer. Remember that most scenery is viewed from a distance. Don't spend time laboring over minute detail that an audience will not see.

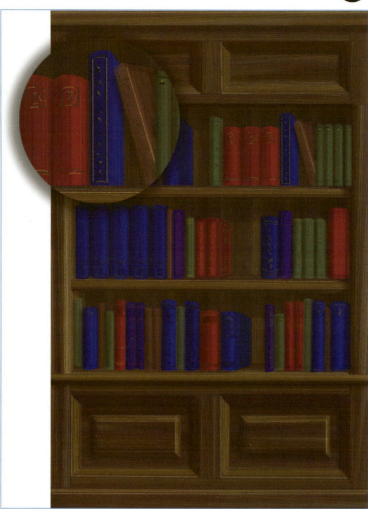

Scale, 2 units wide × 3 units high.

STEP 3
Add Detail

Writing and other details are on the books.

- Carefully consider choices for writing and detail on the books. (See NOTES.)

- Use **Book detail #1** yellow ochre and a small brush to paint detail on the books. This paint contains a substantial amount of water.

- Use a straightedge when appropriate.

- This is a very subtle paint application.

Continue with the other colors.

- Use **Book detail #2** burnt umber and **Book detail #3** black to paint additional detail.

- The techniques previously explained also apply to this application.

Titles in **bold** indicate paint names found on the elevation.

NOTES

- Choices for writing on stage should be decided with care. Consider this example: A rental drop arrived for a production of "Guys and Dolls." On the alley drop a small notice was posted. It read "Harry Potter for President" and was readable in the first row of the theatre. The production was set in the 1950s, long before the character Harry was born.

- Designing and painting scenery with lettering can be a risky choice. Members of the audience should not spend their time in the theatre trying to read the writing on the set. "How good is the acting if the audience looks at writing?" is a reasonable question. Still, help the situation and control the writing on stage when possible.

STEP 4
Shadow

Use **Shadow wash** to paint the shadows.

- Paint a cast shadow in the space between the books.

- Paint a cast shadow at the top of the books. Remember that the books are curved so the shadow will be curved. This cast shadow will only hit the taller books, not this book.

- Carry this shadow into the spaces devoid of books.

- Add a small shadow line at the base of the books. This will help to anchor the books to the shelf. This is a subtle shadow.

- Use a straightedge for the lines when appropriate. Although a straightedge cannot be used to paint curves, it can serve as a guide.

Titles in **bold** indicate paint names found on the elevation.

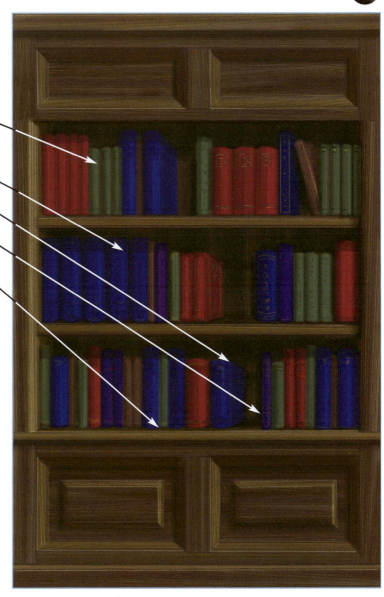

Scale, 2 units wide 3 units high.

NOTES

- Practice mixing and using washes. [ ] d. Washes are used in almost every project. It will take prac

- Please test all paints, especially washes [ ] tend to dry with less intensity and lighter washes will tend to d [ ] ensity (but it is very unpredictable).

- A small flat (maybe 2′ × 3′) will work well as a test flat.

- Stir this paint a lot. It will settle more than paint of regular consistency.

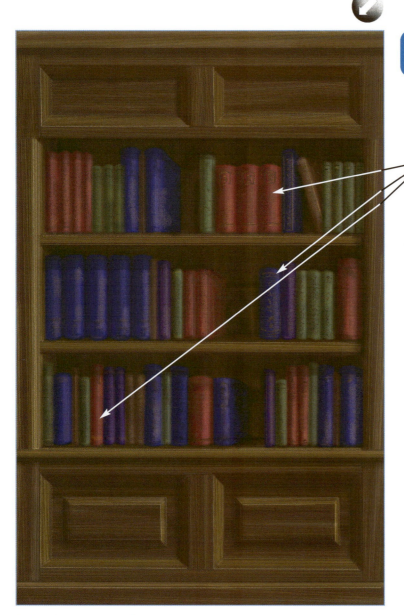

Scale, 2 units wide × 3 units high.

STEP 5
Highlight

Use **Highlight wash** to paint the highlights.

- Paint a sharp highlight on the right side of some of the books. This is the shine seen on some books when illuminated by the light source.
- This is a very subtle highlight.
- Use a straightedge for all these lines

Add final distressing.

- Use **Book detail #1** yellow ochre, **Book detail #2** burnt umber, and **Book detail #3** black to distress the books.
- Experiment with application. Try applying the paint with a brush or a small sponge.
- This application should suggest age on the book.

Titles in **bold** indicate paint names found on the elevation.

NOTES

- **P.S.** Replace a few of the books with other objects frequently found on a bookshelf. Trophies, sculptures, statues, sports memorabilia, decorative boxes, and family items are all possibilities.

- Make this a real challenge and pick items from a specific time period.

Things to Remember

WORK SURFACE

A 4′ × 6′ traditional or hard-covered flat.

TYPE OF PAINT

Rosco *Off Broadway* paint, Rosco *Iddings Deep Colors*, or a commercial latex substitute. See the COLOR SAMPLES page at the beginning of this book for brand and color suggestions.

TYPES OF CONSISTENCY

OUT OF THE CAN—Rosco suggests that the paint can be used right out of the can. This consistency might be thick. Add water to achieve a NORMAL consistency (see below).

NORMAL—Thick enough just to cover other projects in a single coat, assuming that the difference between the paint colors is not too great.

DILUTED—1 or 2 parts paint to 1 part water added to the NORMAL paint consistency.

WATERY—1 part paint to 5 to 10 parts water added to the NORMAL paint consistency. Rosco says: "Diluting with more than 2 parts water may reduce binder strength. Add Rosco *Clear Acrylic Glaze* to restore adhesion and flexibility."

PAINTING TECHNIQUES

BASE PAINT (paint technique)—The first paint color or colors used in a specific painting project, usually the predominant color.

CARTOON—A line drawing of a paint elevation used as a guide for a painting project.

MARBLE (paint technique)—The application of paint in a layer or layers to duplicate the look of marble.

HIGHLIGHT WASH (paint technique)—A light, translucent paint used to represent the reflection of light or an area that receives the greatest amount of illumination.

SHADOW WASH (paint technique)—A dark, transparent paint used to suggest a shadow cast from one object on another.

Glossary

CHAIR RAIL—A horizontal wall trim approximately the height of the top of a chair; used to protect plastered walls from damage caused by the backs of chairs.

BASEBOARD—Molding attached to the bottom of a wall covering the joint of a wall and the adjoining floor.

KRAFT PAPER—Nonabsorbent paper used to protect against spills and protect scenery from additional paint applications.

ROLLED HIGHLIGHT (paint technique)—A translucent highlight with one hard edge and one blended edge to suggest a curved or rounded surface.

ROLLED SHADOW (paint technique)—A translucent shadow with one hard edge and one blended edge to suggest a curved or rounded surface.

STRAIGHTEDGE—A straight length of wood with a handle that ensures the painting of a straight line.

Scale, 2 units wide × 3 units high.

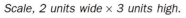

LIGHT DIRECTION

TOOLS NEEDED
(See the Project pages for details.)

- **A collection of scene and housepainting brushes**

- **Chalk or charcoal for cartooning**

- **Tape measure**

- **Straightedge or lining stick**

- **Kraft paper for masking**

Base White	

Marble #1 Gray/green - dark	

Marble #2 Gray - medium	

Marble #3 Pink - medium dark	

Marble #4 Pink - light	

Hightlight wash White/pink - 10% opacity	

Shadow wash Black/violet - 10% opacity	

Wall base Gray - medium light	

Wall spatter Gray - medium dark	

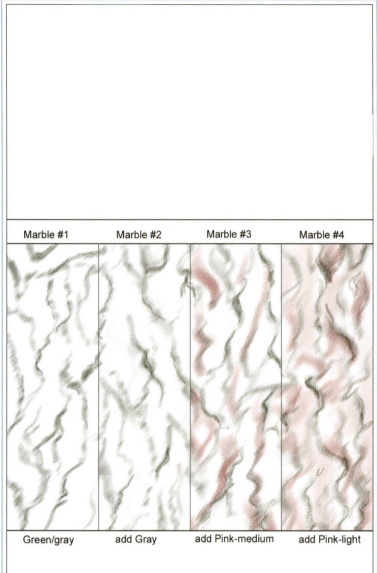

Marble #1 | Marble #2 | Marble #3 | Marble #4

Green/gray | add Gray | add Pink-medium | add Pink-light

Scale, 2 units wide × 3 units high.

- Base paint the flat.
- Use the white **Base** to paint the flat.
- Cover old projects with this paint before painting the marble.
- Allow this to dry completely before painting marble.
- Excess water may reveal old projects.

Painting the marble grain.

- To paint the grain, use **Marble #1**, **Marble #2**, **Marble #3**, and **Marble #4**. Keep the **Base** handy as well.
- Have two buckets of water nearby, one for cleaning brushes and one for splattering clear water.
- The width of the brush is not critical. A brush about 1-1/2″ will work. Keep a natural sponge handy. Use it for blending or soaked up excess water.
- Gather all materials and have them accessible before starting to paint.
- Avoid excess! (See NOTES.)

Titles in **bold** indicate paint names found on the elevation.

IMPORTANT!
- The panel is divided into sections to show the amount of coverage for each of the four color applications.
- *This is an example only!*
- Paint the entire marble area with the first color using the first panel section as an example. Now repeat with the other three colors. See the next page for details.

NOTES

- All things in moderation. Too much water, too much paint, too much time painting, or too much working of the paint will negatively affect the results.

- Painting marble can include many layers and painting techniques. Marble can be painted in a single step. This project falls somewhere in the middle.

- Painting marble with a lot of water on a flat surface can be fun and rewarding. Not all surfaces requiring painted marble are flat. Learn to paint marble without a great deal of water.

- Don't paint or design marble without research. It is amazing the choices of colors that are available.

Things to Remember

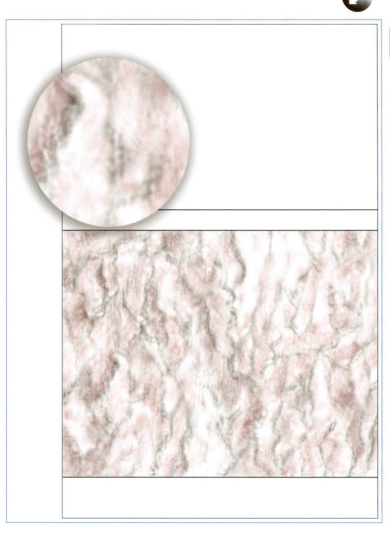

Scale, 2 units wide × 3 units high.

STEP 2
Blend Marble

Lay in the marble colors.

- Before starting to paint, splatter or spray a thin layer of clear water on the area to be painted.

- Paint **Marble #1** on the entire panel area. Use the example on the preceding page to gauge the amount of paint used.

- Use the side of the brush and a light amount of pressure. This is a quick and loose technique.

Repeat this process with **Marble #2**, **Marble #3**, and **Marble #4**.

- Use the example on the preceding page to gauge the amount of paint used. (See NOTES.)

Apply more water.

- Immediately splatter or spray a small amount of water over the area. The paint should begin to blend. (See NOTES.)

- Use a clean brush or a damp sponge to help control the water and help the blending process.

Titles in **bold** indicate paint names found on the elevation.

NOTES
- The grain of the marble is random and should not have a repetitive pattern. Be aware of the painting and avoid repetition of pattern. This will be more difficult to do the larger the painted area becomes.

- Water will blend the paints, but it is also unpredictable and potentially difficult to control.

- If using a traditional muslin-covered flat, excess paint and water might look for the lowest part of the flat. The result could be a mud puddle.

STEP 3
Paint the Baseboard and Chair Rail Trim

Paint the marble for the baseboard.

- Repeat the process to paint the marble at the bottom of the flat.

- Notice that the grain is generally going in a different direction.

- Take care with the amount of water. If tape is used, mask the marble previously painted; excess water will seep under the tape.

- A straightedge can be a barrier. Paint to the straightedge. Don't use any excess water if this is the method of choice.

- The technique must go all the way to the edges of the particular area.

Paint the marble for the chair rail trim.

- Repeat the process to paint the top chair rail marble.

- All of the instructions still apply.

Titles in **bold** indicate paint names found on the elevation.

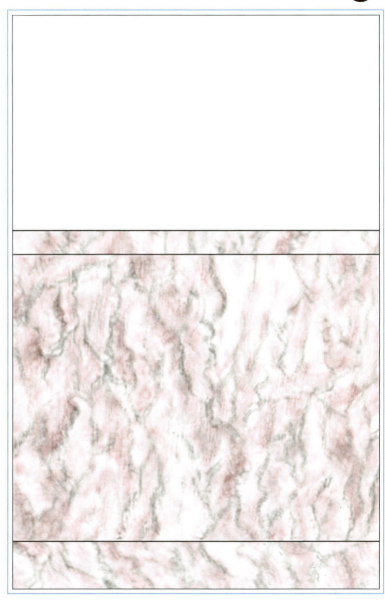

Scale, 2 units wide × 3 units high.

NOTES

- The black cartoon lines are included so it is easier to see the difference between the areas. In fact, white chalk for cartooning this project would be a better choice.

- Some marbles have veins. Others do not, like this project. If the marble being painted has veins, painting them would be the next step.

- Paint the veins on a dry flat with a feather or a small brush.

- A feather is slow but will work well for veining a small amount of marble.

- The side of a thin brush and a little practice will work for larger projects.

- String or cord dipped in paint then dropped on the flat is also a possibility.

- Try various techniques on a test flat before painting the finished work.

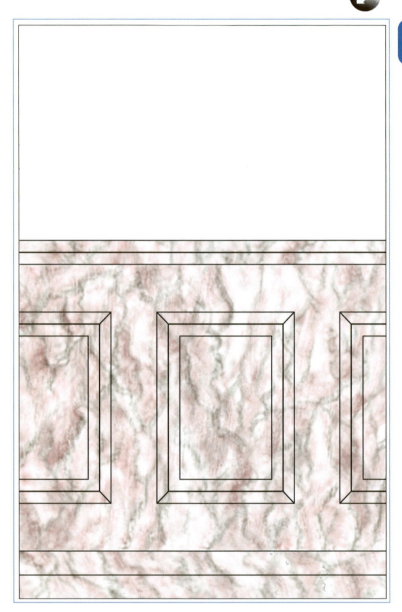

Scale, 2 units wide × 3 units high.

STEP 4
Cartoon the Marble

Use chalk or charcoal to cartoon the flat.

- Please measure very carefully. Many projects are ruined because of mistakes made in measurement.

Consider this:

- Chalk on this light surface might be difficult to see.
- Vine charcoal on this light surface will easily show up; however, the vine charcoal will leave a residue, especially when applied heavily.
- Use the vine charcoal lightly or use chalk for cartooning this example.
- A marker in a lighter color is another possibility.

Titles in **bold** indicate paint names found on the elevation.

NOTES

- When cartooning a flat, use chalk or other light color material on dark surfaces.
- When cartooning a flat, use vine charcoal or other dark material on light surfaces.
- Make sure that whatever is used can be removed or covered up when the cartoon lines are no longer needed.
- Remember, some materials (such as marker) will not always cover with paint. This might be a problem with the current project and might be a real problem when moving to the next project.
- Vine charcoal might leave a residue.

STEP 5
Shadow

Look at the example. Use the **Shadow wash** to paint the shadows.

1. A rolled shadow
2. A cutline
3. A rolled shadow
4. A cutline
5. A shadow straddling the cartoon line

6. A small rolled shadow
7. A cutline
8. Very small cutlines
9. Bevel shadow
10. A cutline
11. A small rolled shadow

12. A weak shadow for separation
13. A cutline
14. A rolled shadow
15. A rolled shadow
16. A cutline

Titles in **bold** indicate paint names found on the elevation.

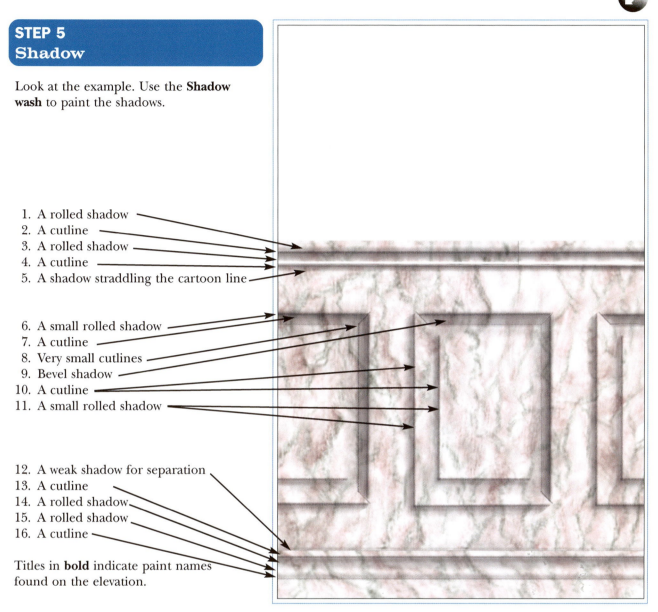

Scale, 2 units wide × 3 units high.

IMPORTANT!
- The **Shadow wash** is critical for success for the project. Please test the paint.

NOTES

- A shadow that fades in intensity on one or both sides is called a "rolled shadow" in this book. The purpose of a rolled shadow is to suggest shadow on a curved surface.

- To achieve this technique:

  - Paint the shadow normally. Immediately clean the brush and paint over the faded side with clean water; *or*

  - Load only one side of the brush that is used for the rolled shadow.

- Practice this technique on the test flat to decide which approach works the best.

- Of course, a straightedge will work for either method.

- All of these instructions are the same for a rolled highlight.

Things to Remember

STEP 6
Highlight

Look at the example. Use the **Highlight wash** to paint the highlights.

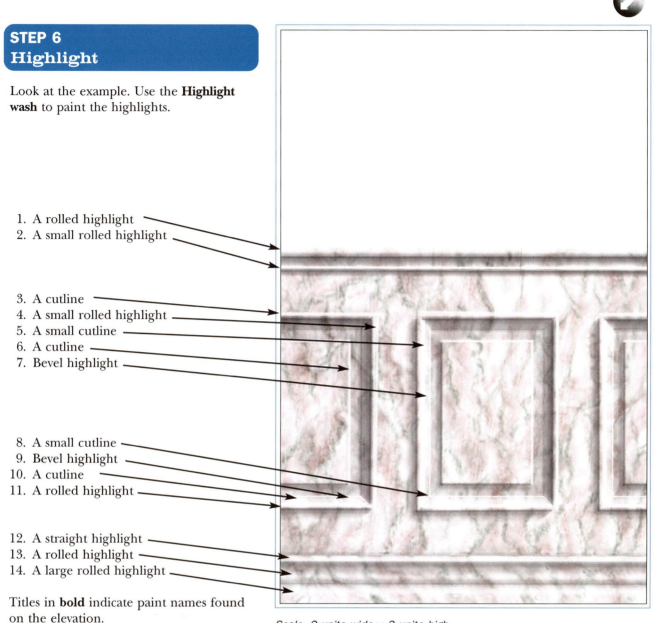

1. A rolled highlight
2. A small rolled highlight

3. A cutline
4. A small rolled highlight
5. A small cutline
6. A cutline
7. Bevel highlight

8. A small cutline
9. Bevel highlight
10. A cutline
11. A rolled highlight

12. A straight highlight
13. A rolled highlight
14. A large rolled highlight

Titles in **bold** indicate paint names found on the elevation.

Scale, 2 units wide × 3 units high.

IMPORTANT!
- The **Highlight wash** is critical for success for the project. Please test the paint.

NOTES
- Practice mixing and using washes. This technique *must* be mastered. Washes are used in almost every project. It will take practice.

- Please test all paints, especially washes. Darker washes will tend to dry with less intensity and lighter washes will tend to dry with more intensity (but it is very unpredictable).

- A small flat (maybe 2′ × 3′) will work well as a test flat.

- Stir this paint often. It will settle more than paint of regular consistency.

Scale, 2 units wide × 3 units high.

STEP 7
Striped Wallpaper

Paint the small piece of striped wallpaper on the very top of the flat. (See NOTES.)

- Base the top of the flat with the **Wall base**.

- Mask off the marble with Kraft paper or lumber.

- Spatter the area with **Marble #2**.

Paint the stripes.

- Mask the area *between the stripes* with Kraft paper or lumber. Make sure the marble is still masked. It would be unfortunate to get spatter on the finished marble.

- Spatter the area again, this time with **Wall spatter**.

- Remove the masking between the stripes.

- Make sure the marble is still masked.

- Spatter the area with **Base**.

Finishing touches.

- Paint a very thin cut line of **Shadow wash** on either side of the stripes.

- Paint a very thin cut line of **Highlight wash** on the right side of the stripes, next to and on the right of the **Shadow wash** line. (See NOTES.)

- Paint a very soft **Shadow wash** line at the bottom of the wallpaper to help separate it from the marble.

Titles in **bold** indicate paint names found on the elevation.

NOTES

- This is a very quick and easy way to paint wallpaper. It might come in handy in a pinch. Altering the size and relationship of the stripes is possible.

- The stripes on the wallpaper are not raised. Painting the shadow and highlight on either side of the wallpaper stripes will help separate them from the background and give them additional interest.

- **P.S.** Try adding a part of a painting on the wall. It could be most any period. Researching painters and their painting will be very interesting. Painting a part of a picture frame will also be a challenge.

Things to Remember

PROJECT 10
Lattice Portal

WORK SURFACE

A 4′ × 6′ traditional or hard-covered flat.

TYPE OF PAINT

Rosco *Off Broadway* paint, Rosco *Iddings Deep Colors*, or a commercial latex substitute. See the COLOR SAMPLES page at the beginning of this book for brand and color suggestions.

TYPES OF CONSISTENCY

OUT OF THE CAN—Rosco suggests that the paint can be used right out of the can. This consistency might be thick. Add water to achieve a NORMAL consistency (see below).

NORMAL—Thick enough just to cover other projects in a single coat, assuming that the difference between the paint colors is not too great.

DILUTED—1 or 2 parts paint to 1 part water added to the NORMAL paint consistency.

WATERY—1 part paint to 5 to 10 parts water added to the NORMAL paint consistency. Rosco says: "Diluting with more than 2 parts water may reduce binder strength. Add Rosco *Clear Acrylic Glaze* to restore adhesion and flexibility."

PAINTING TECHNIQUES

GRADED WET BLEND (paint technique)—To arrange in a scale or series; a smooth blend of colors using a gradation, usually a linear pattern blended together.

CARTOON—A line drawing of a paint elevation used as a guide for a painting project.

DRY BRUSH (paint technique)—Dragging a brush loaded with paint across a dry surface (also called "combing").

HIGHLIGHT WASH (paint technique)—A light, translucent paint used to represent the reflection of light or an area that receives the greatest amount of illumination.

SHADOW WASH (paint technique)—A dark, transparent paint used to suggest a shadow cast from one object on another.

GLOSSARY

GRADIENT—The rate of graded ascent or descent.

LATTICE—A framework or structure of crossed wood or metal strips.

STRAIGHTEDGE—A straight length of wood with a handle that ensures the painting of a straight line.

ARCH—Curved structural member spanning an opening and serving as a support (as for the wall or other weight above the opening).

RAIL—An element of standard flat construction; the top and bottom pieces of wood used to build a flat frame. Also, an element in any other frame.

STILE—An element of standard flat construction; the side pieces of wood used to build a flat frame. Also, an element in any other frame.

CHALK—A stick of soft white or buff limestone composed chiefly of the shells of foraminifers.

CHARCOAL (VINE)—A stick of fine charred softwood used in drawing.

Scale, 2 units wide × 3 units high.

TOOLS NEEDED
(See the Project pages for details.)

- **A collection of scene and housepainting brushes**

- **Chalk or charcoal for cartooning**

- **Tape measure**

- **Straightedge or lining stick**

- **String or trammel points for arcs**

	Gradient #1 — Pthalo blue		Lattice lay-in — Cool gray - medium		Lattice dry brush #3 — French gray - very light
	Gradient #2 — Pthalo blue - medium		Lattice dry brush #1 — French gray - medium		Shadow wash — Black/violet - 10% opacity
	Gradient #3 — Pthalo blue - light		Lattice dry brush #2 — French gray - light		Highlight wash — White - 30% opacity

103

Paint in this area
GRADIENT #1

Paint in this area
A blend of **GRADIENT #1** and **GRADIENT #2**

Paint in this area
GRADIENT #2

Paint in this area
A blend of **GRADIENT #2** and **GRADIENT #3**

Paint in this area
GRADIENT #3

Scale, 2 units wide × 3 units high.

STEP 1
Gradient Background

Prepare the paint used for the graded wet blend: **Gradient #1**, **Gradient #2**, and **Gradient #3**.

- These paints should be NORMAL consistency. Avoid mixing large quantities of paint for this step. The sum of the three colors combined should be only a little more quantity than is needed to base the entire flat. (See NOTES.)

The purpose of the graded wet blend is to achieve an even progression from one color to another.

- Divide the flat into three horizontal sections.
- The bottom section is the largest.
- Base the top section with **Gradient #1**.
- Base the middle section with **Gradient #2**. These paints should almost meet in the blended area.

Now blend these two colors before the paint has a chance to dry.

- Use a clean, damp brush for the blending.
- Work quickly and use a light stroke.
- Don't overwork this technique.

Repeat this procedure with the next two areas and use **Gradient #2** and **Gradient #3**. (See NOTES.)

Titles in **bold** indicate paint names found on the elevation.

NOTES

- Mixing equal parts of **Gradient #1** and **Gradient #3** will produce **Gradient #2**. When the paint is correctly mixed, place a drop of one color into the other buckets to judge their relationship. A drop of the other colors will not affect the original color of the paint.

- If **Gradient #2** is dry when beginning to blend **Gradients #2** and **#3**, re-base the bottom of section two with **Gradient #2**.

- If brush strokes are noticeable and too rough after the blend, smooth out this area. While the paint is still wet, use a clean, damp 4″ brush to gently blend the paint on a horizontal line.

- A graded wet blend can be a difficult technique to master.

- Always have a bucket or two of clean water.

Things to Remember

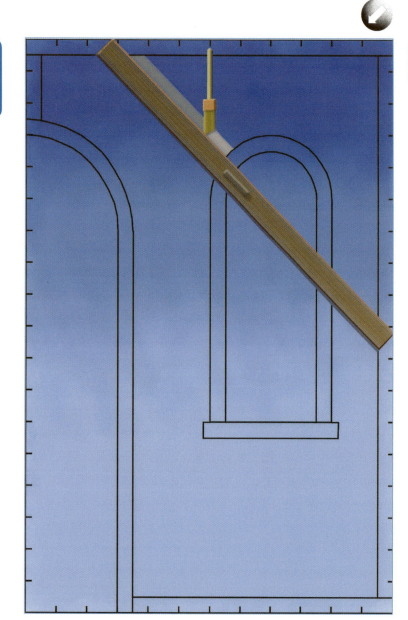

Scale, 2 units wide × 3 units high.

STEP 2
Cartoon the Flat

Use chalk or charcoal to cartoon the flat. All the parts of the frame are 2″ wide.

- Cartoon the arched doorway and the arched window frame. Use string tied to the chalk or charcoal to draw the arcs.

- Cartoon the window sill and the rails (the top and bottom pieces of the frame).

- Now cartoon the stiles (the side pieces of the frame).

- Last, put a register mark every 4″ around all the sides of the flat.

- Layout is challenging for this project. It is easy to get confused when measuring and lining up the straightedge on the register mark. *Concentrate!*

Use the register marks on the perimeter of the flat when painting the lattice.

- Line up the straightedge at the intersection of the register mark and the edge of the flat.

- Start in a corner and always line up and paint on the same side of the straightedge.

- Use a 1-1/2″ brush to paint the slats of the lattice.

Titles in **bold** indicate paint names found on the elevation.

IMPORTANT!
- The marks on the example are quite large to make them easier to see. They should be very small when marked on the actual flat.

10

NOTES

- Although not apparent, the layout for this project can be challenging.

- It is easy to use the incorrect mark when painting on the diagonal. All the marks look similar.

- If layout seems to be an effort, try painting a portion of the dried flat with clean water. Check for accuracy before the water dries. This will take extra time, but less time then having to start the project over again.

- Always line up the straightedge with the intersection of the edge of the flat and the tick mark.

- Always line up and paint the dry brush on the same side of the stick.

Things to Remember

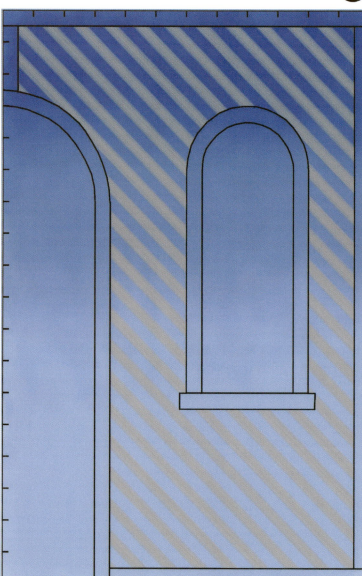

Scale, 2 units wide × 3 units high.

STEP 3
Dry Brush the Back Slats of the Lattice

Use a 1-1/2″ brush to paint the **Lattice lay-in**. This will be a dry brush technique. (See NOTES.)

- Use a straightedge and register marks as explained on the previous page.

- The consistency of the paint should have a little more water than NORMAL.

- Paint each slat as far as possible before lifting the brush or running out of paint. Lift gradually to avoid a visible line when stopping and starting.

- Small variation in the dry brush is desirable.

- This is a dry brush technique. Don't cover the gradient completely.

Use a 1-1/2″ brush to paint **Lattice dry brush #1** on top of the **Lattice lay-in**. This will be a dry brush technique.

- The techniques previously explained also apply to this dry brush.

- Don't cover the first dry brush completely.

Of course, use a straightedge for this painting.

- Be very careful not to paint the cartooned frame or the open areas in the window and door opening.

Titles in **bold** indicate paint names found on the elevation.

NOTES
- A brand new and well cared for brush is not the best choice for the dry brush technique in this project.

- Please take care of paint brushes. Even with proper care, brushes will age and bristles will begin to separate. Don't throw away these brushes. They will work very well for this type of dry brush, spattering, and other painting techniques.

- Cut into the bristles of a new and inexpensive brush if an old brush is not available. This technique will ruin the brush for other applications.

- Inexpensive, disposable bristled brushes are great tools for painting this type of dry brush technique.

Things to Remember

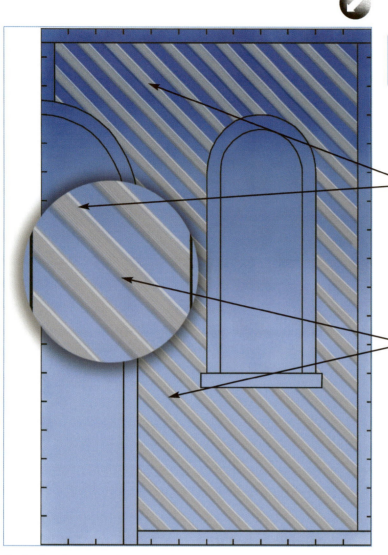

Scale, 2 units wide × 3 units high.

STEP 4
Highlight and Shadow the Back Slats of the Lattice

Add the highlight.

- Mix the **Highlight wash** and use it to paint a sharp highlight on the top of the lattice slats. This is the edge of the lattice slats illuminated by the light source.

- This line is thin.

- Use a straightedge for all these lines.

- It is desirable for the brush to skip when painting this highlight.

Add the shadow.

- Mix the **Shadow wash** and use it to paint a shadow line at the bottom of the lattice slats.

- The shadow wash should be half on and half off the edge of the lattice. The shadow on the lattice will read as a thickness, and the shadow off the lattice will read as the cast shadow.

- Use a straightedge for all these lines.

Titles in **bold** indicate paint names found on the elevation.

NOTES

- Practice mixing and using shadow and highlight washes. It is important to master this skill. Highlight and shadow washes are used for every project. It will take practice.

- Please test all paints, especially washes. Darker washes will tend to dry with less intensity and lighter washes will tend to dry with more intensity (but it is very unpredictable).

- Stir this paint on a regular basis. The pigment will settle more than paint of NORMAL consistency.

- A small flat (maybe 2′ × 3′) will work well as a test flat.

STEP 5
Dry Brush the Front Slats of the Lattice

Use a 1-1/2″ brush to paint the **Lattice lay-in**. This will be a dry brush technique.

- Use a straightedge and register marks in the same way as for the first lattice.

- The consistency of the paint should have a little more water than NORMAL; however, the **Lattice lay-in** should cover most of the first set of slats.

- Paint each slat as long as possible before lifting the brush or running out of paint. Lift gradually to avoid a visible line when stopping and starting.

- Small variations in the dry brush are desirable.

- This is a dry brush technique. Don't cover the gradient completely.

Use a 1-1/2″ brush to paint **Lattice dry brush #1** on top of the **Lattice lay-in**. This will be a dry brush technique.

- The techniques previously explained also apply to this dry brush.

- Don't cover the first dry brush completely.

Of course, use a straightedge for this painting.

- Be very careful not to paint the cartooned frame or the open areas in the window and door opening.

Titles in **bold** indicate paint names found on the elevation.

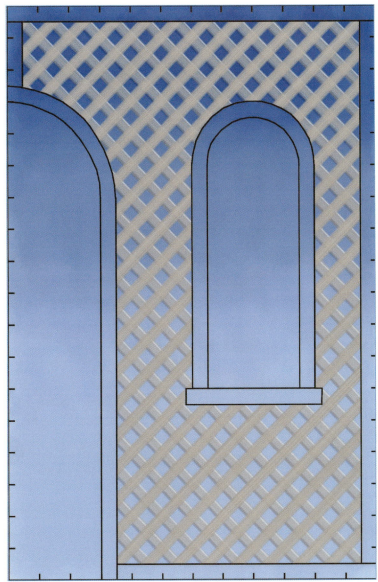

Scale, 2 units wide × 3 units high.

10

NOTES

- Finding adequate working space is important. In situations where space is at a premium, working and storage space is even more essential.

- Find or build shelves for storing paint cans. Paint cans not properly stored and sealed will dry out or, worse, get kicked over.

- Brushes must be thoroughly cleaned and stored hanging up or flat on an open rack. Old and worn brushes can still be used for certain paint applications. Brushes with gobs of dried paint in them are no longer useful.

- Pride in equipment and environment will lead to pride in the work.

Things to Remember

STEP 6
Highlight the Front Slats of the Lattice

Add the highlight.

- Mix the **Highlight wash** and use it to paint a sharp highlight on the top of the lattice slats. This is the edge of the lattice slats illuminated by the light source.

- This line is thin.

- Use a straightedge for all these lines.

- It is desirable for the brush to skip when painting this highlight.

Add the shadow.

- Mix the **Shadow wash** and use it to paint a shadow line at the bottom of the lattice slats.

- The shadow wash should be half on and half off the edge of the lattice. The shadow on the lattice will read as a thickness, and the shadow off the lattice will read as the cast shadow.

- Use a straightedge for all these lines.

Titles in **bold** indicate paint names found on the elevation.

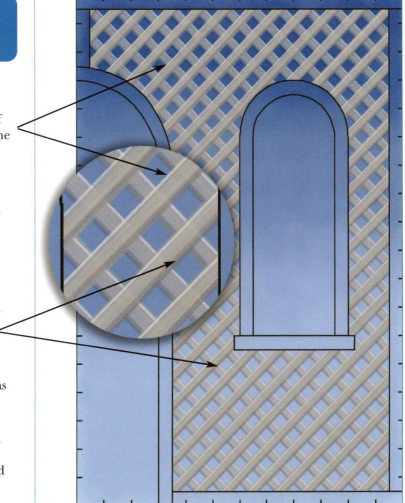

Scale, 2 units wide × 3 units high.

NOTES
- Rules involving eating and drinking while working should be established.

- Treats can add to the enjoyment of the work and the project, but accidents involving food and beverages can be serious.

- Spilled liquids and dropped food can ruin work and equipment.

- Occasional breaks that allow for eating and drinking in nonwork areas might be a good policy.

- Many theatres allow only water in sealed containers in any work or performance spaces in the theatre.

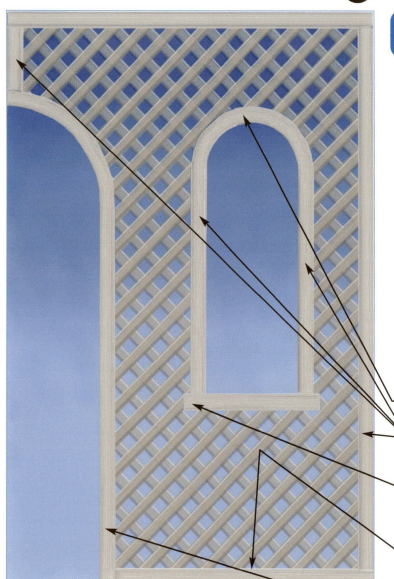

Scale, 2 units wide × 3 units high.

STEP 7
Paint the Lattice Frame

Use a 2″ brush to paint the **Lattice lay-in** and **Lattice dry brush #3** colors.

- The consistency of the paint should have a little more water than NORMAL.

- Paint each frame piece as far as possible before lifting the brush or running out of paint. Lift gradually to avoid a visible line when stopping and starting.

- Use a straightedge to paint all the parts of the frame except for the curves.

It is important that the dry brush technique goes all the way to the ends of the boards. Following the procedure outlined below will avoid failing to do so.

- Paint the *window arch*. Dry brush both colors, one at a time.

- Paint the *stiles* (the side pieces of the frame). Dry brush both colors, one at a time.

- Paint the *window sill*. Dry brush both colors, one at a time. This will cover the bottom of the already-painted window arch.

- Paint the *rails* (the top and bottom pieces of the frame). Dry brush both colors, one at a time. This will cover the end of the already-painted stiles.

- Paint the *arched door*. Dry brush both colors, one at a time. This will cover the left end of the bottom rail and the bottom of the left stile.

Titles in **bold** indicate paint names found on the elevation.

NOTES

- Mood and attitude affect the quality of scene painting. Plan ahead and try to avoid a last-minute rush.

- How long should it take to paint a project? Each painter is different, so there is no one correct answer. Remember that most scenery is viewed from a distance. Don't spend time laboring over minute detail that an audience will not see.

- Many painters find that working with others is more enjoyable then painting alone.

- Music is often a good choice as long as it doesn't interfere with work or with communication. Consider rotating the choice of music selections among all of the workers.

Things to Remember

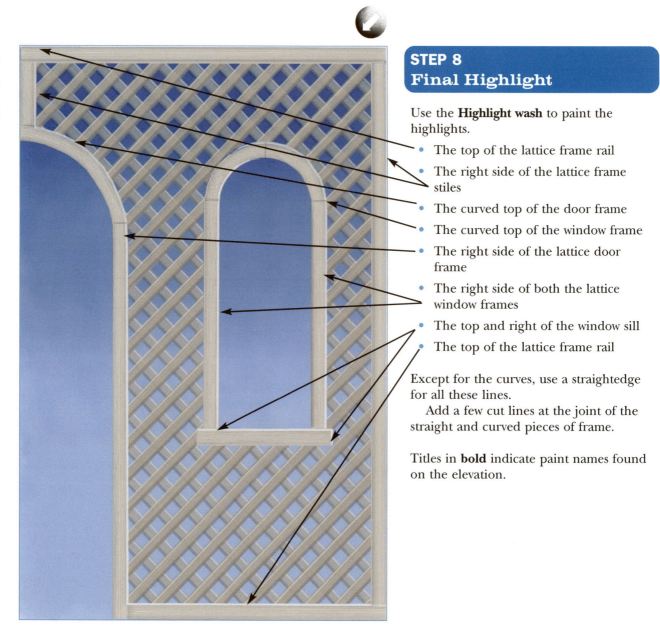

STEP 8
Final Highlight

Use the **Highlight wash** to paint the highlights.

- The top of the lattice frame rail
- The right side of the lattice frame stiles
- The curved top of the door frame
- The curved top of the window frame
- The right side of the lattice door frame
- The right side of both the lattice window frames
- The top and right of the window sill
- The top of the lattice frame rail

Except for the curves, use a straightedge for all these lines.

Add a few cut lines at the joint of the straight and curved pieces of frame.

Titles in **bold** indicate paint names found on the elevation.

Scale, 2 units wide × 3 units high.

NOTES

- Always use a straightedge for painting straight lines.

- It is tempting not to use a straightedge when painting small areas, but speed and quality will improve with the use of a straightedge.

- How long should it take to paint a project? Each painter is different, so there is no one correct answer. Remember that most scenery is viewed from a distance. Don't spend time laboring over minute detail that an audience will not see.

STEP 9
Final Shadow

Use the **Shadow wash** to paint the shadows:

- The bottom of the lattice frame rail
- The top rail and the right stile will cast a shadow on the adjoining lattice slats
- The left side of the lattice frame stile
- The curved bottom of the door frame
- The left side and curve of both the lattice window frames
- The left side of the lattice door frame
- Use a straightedge for all these lines except for the curves
- The window will cast a shadow on the adjoining lattice slats
- The window sill will cast a shadow on the adjoining lattice slats
- The lattice slats that appear to be on top will cast shadows on the lattice slats that appear to be in the rear
- When painting a cast shadow, remember that the lattice slats that appear to be in the rear will get more cast shadow. That is because they are farther away from the object creating the shadow

Titles in **bold** indicate paint names found on the elevation.

Scale, 2 units wide × 3 units high.

NOTES
- **P.S.** The list of additions to this project is long.
- Foliage Is a good choice (see the next project, a continuation of this project). Other types of flowers and plants could be interesting choices.
- Organic material (plants of all sorts) could be regional and specific for the area.
- The lattice in this project is new, or at least in good condition. Distressing or even breaking pieces of the lattice and frame is possible.
- This project could be painted on top of another project, possibly Project 7 (Weathered Wood).

Foliage Added to Lattice

WORK SURFACE

A 4′ × 6′ traditional or hard-covered flat.

TYPE OF PAINT

Rosco *Off Broadway* paint, Rosco *Iddings Deep Colors*, or a commercial latex substitute. See the COLOR SAMPLES page at the beginning of this book for brand and color suggestions.

TYPES OF CONSISTENCY

OUT OF THE CAN—Rosco suggests that the paint can be used right out of the can. This consistency might be thick. Add water to achieve a NORMAL consistency (see below).

NORMAL—Thick enough just to cover other projects in a single coat, assuming that the difference between the paint colors is not too great.

DILUTED—1 or 2 parts paint to 1 part water added to the NORMAL paint consistency.

WATERY—1 part paint to 5 to 10 parts water added to the NORMAL paint consistency. Rosco says: "Diluting with more than 2 parts water may reduce binder strength. Add Rosco *Clear Acrylic Glaze* to restore adhesion and flexibility."

PAINTING TECHNIQUES

CARTOON—A line drawing of a paint elevation used as a guide for a painting project.

FOLIAGE—A representation of leaves, flowers, and branches for architectural ornamentation.

SHADOW WASH (paint technique)—A dark, transparent paint used to suggest a shadow cast from one object on another.

GLOSSARY

RHODODENDRON—Widely cultivated shrubs and trees with large, leathery leaves and showy flowers.

DAFFODIL—A plant whose flowers have a large corona elongated into a trumpet shape.

LATTICE—A framework or structure of crossed wood or metal strips.

HIGHLIGHT—The application of a higher value of color in an attempt to create the illusion of dimension.

CHALK—A stick of soft white or buff limestone composed chiefly of the shells of foraminifers.

CHARCOAL (VINE)—A stick of fine charred softwood used in drawing.

GRADED WET BLEND (paint technique)—To arrange in a scale or series; a smooth blend of colors using a gradation, usually a linear pattern blended together.

PAINT ELEVATION—A scaled, color drawing or painting of a piece of scenery provided by the scenic designer.

TEST FLAT—A wooden frame secured with plywood fasteners and covered with material; built like a traditional flat but smaller.

PARTS OF A BRUSH—The handle, ferrule (the metal band that holds the bristles), and bristles.

ARCH—Curved structural member spanning an opening and serving as a support (as for the wall or other weight above the opening).

ROLLING (paint technique)—Applying paint with a roller; the texture of the roller cover will show when a dryer roller is used.

Scale, 2 units wide × 3 units high.

LIGHT DIRECTION

TOOLS NEEDED
(See the Project pages for details.)

- **A collection of scene and housepainting brushes**

- **Chalk or charcoal for cartooning**

- **Tape measure**

- **Straightedge or lining stick**

 Branch base
Burnt umber

 Branch dark
Raw umber/black

 Branch light
Raw sienna

 Foliage #1
Emerald green/yellow

Foliage #2
Emerald green

 Foliage #3
Chrome oxide green - light

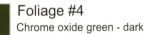 **Foliage #4**
Chrome oxide green - dark

 Foliage #5
Purple - dark

 Daffodil #1
Lemon yellow - very light

 Daffodil #2
Lemon yellow - medium light

 Daffodil #3
Lemon yellow

 **Daffodil #4**
Yellow ochre/lemon yellow

 **Shadow wash**
Black/violet - 10% opacity

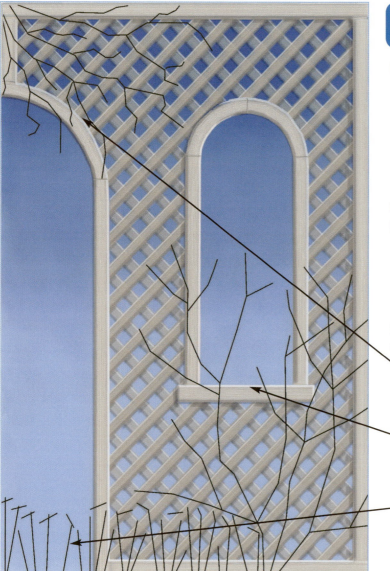

Scale, 2 units wide × 3 units high.

STEP 1
Cartoon the Flat

Use chalk or charcoal to cartoon the flat.

- Please measure very carefully. Many projects are ruined because of mistakes made in measurement.

- Use the lattice as a grid to find the location of the branches, assuming the lattice is painted correctly.

If the lattice project was not previously painted:

- Choose a base color and technique.

- Measure or use the grid method to transfer the foliage cartooning. (See NOTES.)

Make every attempt to copy the cartooning for the branches and foliage.

- The cartooning for the vine branches in the upper left corner is drawn with a single line representing each branch.

- The rhododendron contains three branches that overlap. Draw all the branches, but paint them in order from back to front.

- Cartoon the daffodils across the bottom. An option would be to cartoon these after painting the rhododendron and after the paint is dry.

Titles in **bold** indicate paint names found on the elevation.

NOTES

- A grid is a series of vertical and horizontal lines placed on or over a paint elevation.

- A corresponding grid with the same number of boxes is placed on or over the flat.

- Transfer the line information from the grid on the paint elevation to the larger grid on the flat.

- A grid is a useful method for cartooning when the shapes drawn are natural and nonarchitectural.

- A grid can be chalk or charcoal lines snapped on the flat. It can also be string secured with "T" pins around the perimeter of the flat; no lines to erase is an advantage of this method.

- The colored chalk found in most shop snap lines will be difficult to remove from the flat. A new snap line filled with charcoal or chalk power should be an addition to the scene painting equipment.

Things to Remember

Scale, 2 units wide × 3 units high.

STEP 2
Paint Background Foliage

For this step use **Foliage #4**, **Foliage #3**, and **Foliage #2**.

- When the paint color is correctly mixed, place a drop of one color into the other buckets. This will give a visual clue if the paint is mixed properly. A small drop of the other colors won't affect the paint.

- Mix all paint colors for a single project at the same time. If that is not possible, mix a group of colors in a single session—all of the foliage paint colors in this project, for example.

Start with the darkest color, **Foliage #4**.

- Develop a brush stroke that works for the leaf painting.

Now would be a great time to consider the use of a test flat to develop a brush stroke that will work for leaves. Experiment with multiple brushes and techniques. Please test before painting!

- Paint a group of leaves at the same time.

- Start the leaf at the outside and work toward the center of the group of leaves.

Repeat with **Foliage #3** and **Foliage #2**.

Titles in **bold** indicate paint names found on the elevation.

NOTES

- If paint is used in a single painting session, a small, open plastic bucket will work nicely. They can be purchased in various sizes and are affordable; many also include lids.

- If paint is used for an extended period of time, mix and store it in a closed container. Use an empty paint can if it is clean. They work well and they are free. Remove the labels from old paint cans to avoid confusion with paint stock.

- Attach a piece of tape to the side of a dry paint can or bucket and write the color and project on it.

- Labeling is important when in a class or in a shop with multiple shows in production.

- The containers for a popular brand of crystal cat litter work great for storing and using paint. The containers are clear; have a built-in handle, wide mouth, and screw-on top; and come in two sizes.

Things to Remember

11

STEP 3
Paint the Branches

Paint the vines on the upper left part of the flat. Use the **Branch base**, **Branch dark**, and **Branch light** paint colors.

- Paint over cartoon lines with the **Branch base** paint. Use a 1″ to 2″ brush. (See NOTES.)

- Use the **Branch light** paint, the same brush, and the same technique. Keep in mind the direction of the light. Paint the side of the branches toward the light.

- Now use the **Branch dark** paint, the same brush, and the same technique. Keep in mind the direction of the light. Paint the side of the branches away from the light.

The three branches on the rhododendron overlap.

- Paint the middle branch bark with the three colors, one at a time.

- Paint the left branch bark with the three colors, one at a time. Portions of this branch cross over the center branch.

- Finally, paint the right branch bark with the three colors, one at a time. Portions of this branch cross over the center branch.

- These branches are a little wider than the vines.

- Use the same approach and technique used for painting the vines.

Titles in **bold** indicate paint names found on the elevation.

Scale, 2 units wide × 3 units high.

NOTES
- This painting technique is like a dry brush technique.

- Use the side of the brush instead of the width of the brush.

- A wider brush will hold more paint.

- The width of the brush should not matter if the edge of the brush is thin.

- This is a fast, sketchy technique. Keep it loose.

STEP 4
Paint the Dark
Foliage Colors

When painting foliage, begin with the darker colors. Have **Foliage #5** and **Foliage #4** handy.

Paint the vine leaves.

- Use **Foliage #5** to paint the first set of leaves on the vine.

- Use a brush that will produce a small brush stroke.

- After this dries, repeat the process with **Foliage #4**.

Paint the rhododendron leaves.

- Use **Foliage #5** to paint the leaves on the rhododendron.

- Use a brush that will produce a longer brush stroke than the leaves on the vine.

- Don't cover up the leaves behind the branches.

- After this application of paint dries, repeat the process with **Foliage #4**.

Titles in **bold** indicate paint names found on the elevation.

Scale, 2 units wide × 3 units high.

IMPORTANT!
- Refer to page 127 for a detailed progression of the foliage painting technique.

11

> **NOTES**
>
> - There are many different types of foliage, trees, and plants.
>
> - Research the kind of foliage to paint if you are in a position to make that choice.
>
> - Plant encyclopedias can be very large and expensive but provide a great amount of information.
>
> - Smaller, more specific books on select topics have fewer pages and are more affordable.
>
> - A library should have a great selection of horticultural books.
>
> - This information is also available online.
>
> - It is always easier to paint specific elements. Making up a type of foliage to paint is difficult.

Things to Remember

The progression of painting foliage is pictured below. In general, work from back to front and from dark to light.

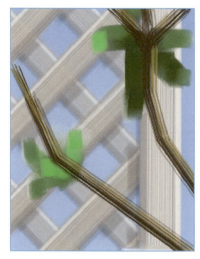

Phase one. A few of the leaves are behind the branches. Paint leaves first (Step 2). Next paint the branches on top (see Step 3).

Phase two. Add **Foliage #5** (see Step 4).

Phase three. Add **Foliage #4** (see Step 4).

Phase four. Add **Foliage #3** (see Step 5).

Phase five. Add **Foliage #2** (see Step 5).

Phase six. Add **Foliage #1** and seed detail (see Step 6).

11

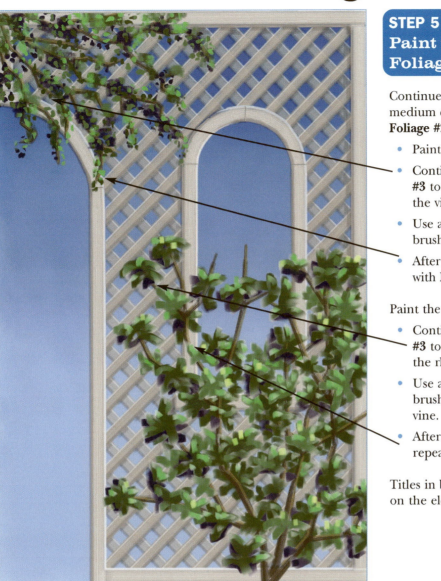

Scale, 2 units wide × 3 units high.

STEP 5
Paint the Medium Foliage Colors

Continue painting foliage with the medium colors. Have **Foliage #3** and **Foliage #2** ready.

- Paint the vine leaves.
- Continue the technique with **Foliage #3** to paint the next set of leaves on the vine. (See NOTES.)
- Use a brush that will produce a small brush stroke.
- After this dries, repeat the process with **Foliage #2**.

Paint the rhododendron leaves.

- Continue the technique with **Foliage #3** to paint the first set of leaves on the rhododendron. (See NOTES.)
- Use a brush that will produce a longer brush stroke than the leaves on the vine.
- After this application of paint dries, repeat the process with **Foliage #2**.

Titles in **bold** indicate paint names found on the elevation.

NOTES

- The lighter colors are applied to progressively fewer leaves.
- The lighter colors should reflect the direction of the light and how that light reacts with the leaves.

STEP 6
Paint the Light Foliage Color and the Detail

Finish painting foliage with the lightest color. Use **Foliage #1**.

- Paint the vine leaves.
- Finish the technique with **Foliage #1** to paint the final set of leaves on the vine. (See NOTES.)
- Use a brush that will produce a small brush stroke.

Paint the rhododendron leaves.

- Finish the technique by using **Foliage #1** to paint the first set of leaves on the rhododendron. (See NOTES.)
- Use a brush that will produce a longer brush stroke.

Add detail. Use the **Branch base**, **Branch dark**, and **Branch light** paint colors.

- Use the same technique for the branches to paint the seeds.
- Use the edge of a brush. Paint quickly with a loose hand.
- Use the same technique for the leaves to paint the dead leaves. The **Branch base**, **Branch dark**, and **Branch light** paint colors are needed.

Titles in **bold** indicate paint names found on the elevation.

Scale, 2 units wide × 3 units high.

NOTES

- A stamp is another way to paint foliage, especially on a large scale. Cut pieces of 1/2″ foam in the desired shape. Glue these on a piece of plywood, lauan, or Masonite® (hardboard). Attach a dowel to the side opposite the foam pieces. The dowel can be inserted into the end of a bamboo stick extension.

- Turn the stamp and press on different areas of the stamp to get varied shapes of leaves.

- A cafeteria tray works well for loading paint on a stamp. A small amount of paint at a time is desirable.

- Test this application method before painting on scenery.

11

STEP 7
Paint the Dark Daffodil Foliage Colors

Start with the darker colors as with the other foliage. Have **Foliage #5** and **Foliage #4** handy.

* Paint the daffodil leaves.
* Use **Foliage #5** to paint the first set of leaves for the daffodil.
* Use a larger size brush (about 1-1/2" wide) to lay in these colors. Work quickly.
* After this application of paint dries, repeat the process with **Foliage #4**.

Titles in **bold** indicate paint names found on the elevation.

Scale, 2 units wide × 3 units high.

NOTES

* Using a textured roller cover is another method for painting foliage. Cut a leaf pattern into a foam roller cover or glue pieces of foam onto the core of a roller. This pattern will tend to be small because of the size of the roller cover.

* Turn the roller and change the pressure of the roller to get varied shapes of leaves.

* A cafeteria tray works well for loading paint on a roller. A small amount of paint at a time is desirable.

* Test this application method before painting on scenery.

STEP 8
Paint the Light Daffodil Foliage Colors and Flowers

Continue painting foliage with the medium colors. Use **Foliage #3**, **Foliage #2**, and **Foliage #1**.

Paint the daffodil leaves.

- Continue the technique with **Foliage #3** to paint the next set of leaves on the daffodil.

- Use a brush about 1″ wide.

- After this dries, repeat the process with **Foliage #2**.

- After this dries, repeat the process with **Foliage #1**. Paint sparingly. Use this for only the brightest part of a leaf.

- The lighter colors should reflect the direction of the light and how that light will react with the leaves.

Start with **Daffodil #3** and base the flower areas. Keeping in mind the direction of the light, use:

- **Daffodil #4** to paint the darkest areas of the flower.

- **Daffodil #2** to paint the lighter areas of the flower.

- **Daffodil #1** to paint the brightest areas of the flowers. This color functions as highlight. (See detail in the example.)

Titles in **bold** indicate paint names found on the elevation.

Scale, 2 units wide × 3 units high.

11

NOTES

- Scene painting brushes are expensive, aren't they? Always leave enough time at the end of a painting session for proper cleanup, especially brush cleanup.

- Don't soak paint brushes. Soaking can cause bristles to droop, ferrules to rust, and handles to swell.

- Use lukewarm water and a mild soap to clean brushes.

- A wire brush can harm the bristles and even pull them out from the ferrule. Use a brush comb specifically intended for fine brushes.

- Place the brush back in its plastic keeper. If the brush did not come in one, use a piece of paper towel to gently wrap the bristles.

Things to Remember

STEP 9
Shadow

Prepare the paint used for the **Shadow wash**.

- The consistency of the paint should be WATERY.
- Consider adding additional binder.
- Please test. (See NOTES.)

Use about a 1″ brush to paint the foliage cast shadow.

- Paint the cast shadow from the foliage on the lattice and frame.
- When painting cast shadows, keep the bottom edge of the brush parallel with the light direction. This will automatically line up the shadows with the direction of the light.

Titles in **bold** indicate paint names found on the elevation

Scale, 2 units wide × 3 units high.

NOTES

- Practice mixing and using shadow and highlight washes. It is important to master this skill. Highlight and shadow washes are used for every project. It will take practice.

- Please test all paints, especially washes. Darker washes will tend to dry with less intensity and lighter washes will tend to dry with more intensity (but it is very unpredictable).

- Stir this paint on a regular basis. The pigment will settle more than paint of regular consistency.

- A small flat (maybe 2′ × 3′) will work well as a test flat.

11

Fieldstone and Brownstone

WORK SURFACE

A 4′ × 6′ traditional or hard-covered flat.

TYPE OF PAINT

Rosco *Off Broadway* paint, Rosco *Iddings Deep Colors*, or a commercial latex substitute. See the COLOR SAMPLES page at the beginning of this book for brand and color suggestions.

TYPES OF CONSISTENCY

OUT OF THE CAN—Rosco suggests that the paint can be used right out of the can. This consistency might be thick. Add water to achieve a NORMAL consistency (see below).

NORMAL—Thick enough just to cover other projects in a single coat, assuming that the difference between the paint colors is not too great.

DILUTED—1 or 2 parts paint to 1 part water added to the NORMAL paint consistency.

WATERY—1 part paint to 5 to 10 parts water added to the NORMAL paint consistency. Rosco says: "Diluting with more than 2 parts water may reduce binder strength. Add Rosco *Clear Acrylic Glaze* to restore adhesion and flexibility."

PAINTING TECHNIQUES

BASE PAINT (paint technique)—The first paint color or colors used in a specific painting project, usually the predominant color.

CARTOON—A line drawing of a paint elevation used as a guide for a painting project.

SPATTER (paint technique)—A method of texture using a brush to throw drops of paint on a surface.

SCUMBLE (paint technique)—Blending two or more random patches of color. Size of the patches and the amount of blend will vary depending on the project.

WASH—Paint that has been thinned to achieve transparency.

SPONGING (paint technique)—Creating a texture by applying paint with a sponge.

DRY BRUSH (paint technique)—Dragging a brush loaded with paint across a dry surface (also called "combing")

HIGHLIGHT WASH (paint technique)—A light, translucent paint used to represent the reflection of light or an area that receives the greatest amount of illumination.

Glossary

FIELDSTONE—Stone used on buildings, usually in unaltered form; normally taken from the field.

BROWNSTONE—A reddish brown sandstone used for buildings or dwellings faced with brownstone.

MULLION—Large vertical or radiating members that divide units of a window, door, or screen.

MUNTIN—Small horizontal wood strips that separate and hold each pane of glass in a door or window.

SPONGE, NATURAL (as tool)—An elastic, porous mass of interlacing horny fibers that forms the internal skeleton of various marine animals; when wetted, it is able to absorb water.

STRAIGHTEDGE—A straight length of wood with a handle that ensures the painting of a straight line.

Scale, 2 units wide × 3 units high.

LIGHT DIRECTION

TOOLS NEEDED
(See the Project pages for details.)

- **A collection of scene and housepainting brushes**

- **Chalk or charcoal for cartooning**

- **Tape measure**

- **Straightedge or lining stick**

- **Natural sponge for painting**

Base Raw umber - light	**Fieldstone #1** Yellow ochre - medium	**Fieldstone wash #3** Raw umber - 10% opacity
Spatter #1 Burnt sienna	**Fieldstone #2** Burnt sienna - medium	**Fieldstone wash #4** Black - 10% opacity
Spatter #2 Raw umber	**Fieldstone wash #1** Yellow ochre - 10% opacity	**Shadow wash** Black/violet - 10% opacity
Fieldstone base Raw umber - medium	**Fieldstone wash #2** Burnt sienna - 10%opacity	**Highlight wash** White/raw umber - 10% opacity

135

STEP 1
Base and Spatter

Base paint the flat with the **Base**.

- If this flat is used for a scene painting class, the paint should be just thick enough to cover the previous painting project.

- If this is a new flat, the paint should be just thick enough to cover the flat.

- In either case, remember that a lot of additional paint will go on this flat. Don't use a great deal of paint.

Prepare **Spatter #1** and **Spatter #2**. (See NOTES.)

- The consistency is important. Proper consistency will help the process.

Use a 3″ or 4″ brush to paint the spatter. Use both spatter colors, one at a time.

- Dip the brush in the paint and use the side of the bucket to remove excess paint from the brush, then swipe the brush on the floor or other approved area to remove even more excess.

- Even spatter at this point of the project is not necessary.

Titles in **bold** indicate paint names found on the elevation.

Scale, 2 units wide × 3 units high.

NOTES

- The consistency of the spatter paint should be DILUTED. If the paint is too thick, it will stay on the brush. If the paint is too thin, it will not read very well on the finished flat.

- There are many ways of applying spatter. One method is to hit the spatter brush against a stick or hand to control the application. Flicking the wrist in the direction of the painting surface but avoiding back-snap is another possibility. Wildly swinging the brush is likely to deposit paint on all adjacent surfaces, including coworkers. This will make the supervisors upset.

- This is a small area to spatter. A sprayer can be used for larger projects.

STEP 2
Cartoon the Flat

Use chalk or charcoal to cartoon the flat.

- Please measure very carefully. Many projects are ruined because of mistakes made in measurement.

Make every attempt to copy the fieldstone in the elevation when cartooning the flat. When drawing fieldstone, a number of items are important if the desired result is the look of realistic fieldstone:

- Vertical mortar joints should be staggered as much as possible.
- Avoid huge and oddly shaped areas of mortar. Mortar joints should be as uniform as possible.
- The stone should not be too strangely or oddly shaped.

Titles in **bold** indicate paint names found on the elevation.

Scale, 2 units wide × 3 units high.

12

> ## IMPORTANT!
> - The cartooning in this example is complete, but it is likely that the cartooning will be drawn in stages when actually painting this project. Accurately cartoon the fieldstone at this point. The windows and brownstone can be cartooned after the fieldstone is complete and dry.

12

> **NOTES**
> - When cartooning a flat, use chalk or other light-color material on dark surfaces and use vine charcoal or other dark material on light surfaces.
>
> - Make sure that whatever is used can be removed or covered up with paint when the guides are no longer needed.
>
> - Remember, some materials (such as marker) will not always cover with paint. This might be a problem with the current project and might be a real problem when moving to the next project.

Things to Remember

STEP 3
Mortar Splatter

Splatter with dirty water wash.

- Use **Fieldstone wash** #4 with additional water. Use this paint to splatter the flat. Use less paint with more water for splattering. (See NOTES.)

- The splatter in this example will add texture to the mortar. Although it is not the primary goal, this splatter will also add texture to the fieldstone.

- A little water will help to blend the paint.

- Too much water will cause the paint to puddle together and lose some of the definition.

Titles in **bold** indicate paint names found on the elevation.

Scale, 2 units wide × 3 units high.

IMPORTANT!
- The example on this page has the brownstone and the window areas masked from the splatter for clarity. It will not present a problem in the future of this project if these areas are not masked.

12

> **NOTES**
>
> - There is one letter difference between the words *splatter* and *spatter*. Make sure the technique being communicated is correct. The painting techniques are similar. Think of splatter as spatter with additional water.
>
> - Have a bucket of clear water handy when splattering. If the splatter wash is too heavy and defined, splatter clean water to help defuse and blend the paint.
>
> - Splatter is also called "wet spatter." Calling this technique "wet spatter" might avoid a communication problem.

Things to Remember

STEP 4
Fieldstone Base and Scumble

Prepare the **Fieldstone base, Fieldstone #1**, and **Fieldstone #2** and use these colors for the scumble.

- The consistency should have a little more water than NORMAL paint.

Use about a 2″ brush to paint stones.

- Paint a stone or group of stones with the **Fieldstone base**.

- Apply the two scumble colors, **Fieldstone #1** and **Fieldstone #2**, while the base paint is still wet.

- Work a small group of stones at a time.

- The desired effect should appear rough. Don't overblend these colors.

- Work quickly. This is a very loose, caffeine-aided technique.

- Use one brush to apply each color.

- Look at the example. Notice that the scumble colors are not applied uniformly. Use these colors to begin the process of painting individual stones so they have their own color and texture.

Titles in **bold** indicate paint names found on the elevation.

Scale, 2 units wide × 3 units high.

NOTES

- Scene painting brushes are expensive, aren't they? Always leave enough time at the end of a painting session for proper cleanup, especially for brush cleanup.

- Don't soak paint brushes. Soaking can cause bristles to droop, ferrules to rust, and handles to swell.

- Use lukewarm water and a mild soap to clean brushes.

- A wire brush can harm the bristles and even pull them out from the ferrule. Use a brush comb specifically intended for fine brushes.

- Place the brush back in its plastic keeper. If the brush did not come in one, use a piece of paper towel to gently wrap the bristles.

Scale, 2 units wide × 3 units high.

STEP 5
Fieldstone Washes

Prepare the paint colors used for the fieldstone washes. The washes used for this step are:

- **Fieldstone wash #1**, yellow ochre
- **Fieldstone wash #2**, burnt sienna
- **Fieldstone wash #3**, raw umber
- **Fieldstone wash #4**, black

Note that the consistency of these paints should be WATERY with a bit more pigment or DILUTED with a bit more water.

- Consider adding additional binder.
- Please test. (See NOTES.)

Use about a 1″ brush to paint these colors.

- Although a decision might be made to paint these colors from light to dark, order is not important.
- Make every attempt to follow the example on this page.
- The fieldstones are in the same palette; however, each has its own color and character.
- Use these washes to begin the process of giving the stones dimension through light and shadow.

Titles in **bold** indicate paint names found on the elevation.

NOTES
- Practice mixing and using washes. This technique *must* be mastered. Washes are used in almost every project. It will take practice.

- Please test all paints, especially washes. Darker washes will tend to dry with less intensity and lighter washes will tend to dry with more intensity (but it is very unpredictable).

- A small flat (maybe 2′ × 3′) will work well as a test flat.

- Stir this paint a lot. It will settle more than paint of NORMAL consistency.

STEP 6
Fieldstone Spatter

- Go back and use **Spatter #1** and **Spatter #2**. (See NOTES.)

- The consistency is important. Proper consistency will help the process.

Use a 3″ or 4″ brush to paint the spatter. Use both spatter colors, one at a time.

- Dip the brush in the paint and use the side of the bucket to remove excess paint from the brush, then swipe the brush on the floor or other approved area to remove even more excess.

- The spatter will blend the techniques used up to this point and add texture to the stones.

- The spatter should not be too heavy and should be fairly even.

- Tips and techniques on spattering still apply in this step.

Titles in **bold** indicate paint names found on the elevation.

Scale, 2 units wide × 3 units high.

IMPORTANT!

- The example on this page has the brownstone and the window areas masked from the splatter for clarity. It will not present a problem in the future of this project if these areas are not masked.

NOTES

- The consistency of the spatter paint should be DILUTED. If the paint is too thick, it will stay on the brush. If the paint is too thin, it will not read very well on the finished flat.

- Applying spatter at this time should add more texture to the fieldstone.

- The spatter should also help to blend the techniques used to create the stone up to this point.

- Spatter at this time might not be necessary, so use in moderation.

12

Things to Remember

STEP 7
Fieldstone Highlight and Shadow

Prepare the colors used for the **Shadow wash** and **Highlight wash**.

- The consistency should be WATERY.
- Consider adding additional binder.
- Please test. (See NOTES.)

Paint the highlight and shadow.

- Paint the **Highlight wash** on the parts of the fieldstone that are toward the light.
- Paint the **Shadow wash** on the parts of the fieldstone that are away from the light.
- There will also be some internal highlights and shadows because of the irregular surface of each stone.
- The irregular edges and surfaces on each stone will reflect the highlight and shadow in different ways. (See NOTES.)

Paint the cast shadow.

- Paint the cast shadow on the side of the fieldstone away from the light. This is another shaky technique.

Titles in **bold** indicate paint names found on the elevation.

Scale, 2 units wide × 3 units high.

IMPORTANT!

- *Do not outline the stones in highlight and shadow.*
- There might be a tendency to paint shadow on one side and highlight on the other. Resist the temptation!
- Each stone has an irregular and unique surface. Paint with this fact in mind.

NOTES

- Use about a 1″ brush to paint the fieldstone cast shadow.

- Paint the cast shadow from the fieldstones on the mortar and possibly adjacent stones.

- When painting cast shadows on irregular objects, keep the bottom edge of the brush parallel with the light direction. This will automatically line up the shadows with the direction of the light.

Things to Remember

Scale, 2 units wide × 3 units high.

Window base
Black

Window scumble
Purple

Brownstone base
Burnt umber - medium

Dark sponge
Burnt sienna

Medium sponge
Raw umber - medium

Light sponge
Raw umber - light

Brownstone mortar
Raw umber - light

Dark window frame
Raw umber

Window frame base
Raw umber - medium,

Light window frame
Raw umber - light

Shadow wash
Black/violet - 10% opacity

Highlight wash
White/raw umber - 10% opacity

Scale, 2 units wide × 3 units high.

STEP 8
Window Base and Scumble

Prepare the **Window base** and **Window scumble** paint colors used for the scumble.

- The consistency should have a little more water than NORMAL paint.
- Cartoon the area that will be the window. The window frame and the brownstone meet at this line.
- The example shows the scumble ending at the brownstone at a clean line of paint. The scumble must extend this far.
- It is likely that the scumble will go past this line when actually painted. This is all right. The brownstone and later the window frame will cover the unwanted edges.

Use a 2″ or 3″ brush to paint the window area. (See NOTES.)

- Base paint the window area with the **Window base**.
- While the base is still wet, blend in a small amount of the **Window scumble**.
- Work quickly.
- Don't overwork the blending.
- Cartoon the window and frame when the window scumble is dry.

Titles in **bold** indicate paint names found on the elevation.

NOTES

- In terms of time, scumble should take only a little longer than base painting. Scumble should be a quick technique, and it adds more interest than one color of base paint.

- Two major factors affect the look of scumble: One is the number and contrast of the paint colors, and the second is the size of the brushes used for the technique.

- Have a bucket of clean water nearby. Although this seems obvious, handy clean water will solve a variety of problems.

STEP 9
Brownstone Base and Sponge

Prepare the **Brownstone base** used in this step.

Prepare a small amount of these colors for the sponge texture:

- **Dark sponge**, burnt sienna
- **Medium sponge**, raw umber (medium)
- **Light sponge**, raw umber (light)

It's now time to paint the brownstone.

- Base paint the areas that will be brownstone. Start sponging before the base paint dries.
- Work a small area at a time.

Use a natural sponge for this application.

- Mask the fieldstone area.
- Do not sponge too heavily. Make sure the **Brownstone base** is visible through the sponged paint.
- Remember to rotate the sponge to avoid developing an unwanted pattern.
- Dip the sponge in the paint and remove the excess. Test the paint on another surface before painting the flat.
- Paint all the way to the edge of the brownstone. (See NOTES.)
- **Light sponge** is applied last. Use less of this color than the other sponge colors.

Titles in **bold** indicate paint names found on the elevation.

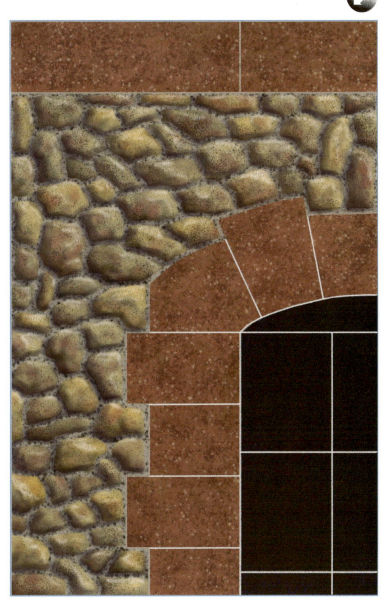

Scale, 2 units wide × 3 units high.

NOTES

- Use a natural sponge for this technique. A small sponge will work for a small project. Applying this technique to a large area will require a large sponge.
- Constantly turn the sponge to avoid developing a pattern.
- Make sure the sponge technique goes all the way to the edges of the area painted. Use a small piece of sponge when working around three-dimensional scenery.
- A synthetic sponge will work well for other techniques.

Scale, 2 units wide × 3 units high.

STEP 10
Window Frame and Mortar

Paint the mullions on the window first.

- Paint over the chalk lines with the **Window frame base** paint color.

- Paint the sides of the mullions toward the light with the **Light window frame** paint color (the right and top of the mullions).

- Paint the sides of the mullions away from the light with the **Dark window frame** paint color (the left and bottom of the mullions). Look at the detail in the example.

Paint the window frame.

- Use the **Window frame base** color to paint the window frame. A semidry brush technique will work well. The areas not covered will appear as wood grain on the painted window trim.

- Paint the edge of the frame toward the light with the **Light window frame** paint color. This is the right side of the vertical frame.

- Paint the edge away from the light with the **Dark window frame** paint color. This is the bottom of the curved frame.

Paint the mortar.

- Use the **Brownstone mortar** to paint a mortar line between the brownstone blocks.

Titles in **bold** indicate paint names found on the elevation.

NOTES

- A wood-grain "rocker" tool is another method of painting wood grain.

- Plastic wood-grain "rocker" tools are popular and can be purchased at most hardware and home improvement stores. A light base is applied and allowed to dry. A darker and more diluted paint is applied on top. A coarse grain is achieved by dragging the tool and simultaneously rocking the tool up and down. It is interesting, even fascinating, the way this tool works.

- The plastic wood-graining tool does have its limitations. The results can lack a certain degree of sophistication without additional painting. Ideally, a smooth, hard surface is required. Sizes can limit effective application.

STEP 11
Final Highlight and Shadow

Mix the colors used for the **Shadow wash** and **Highlight wash**.

- The consistency of the paint should be WATERY.
- Consider adding additional binder.
- Please test. (See NOTES.)

Use about a 1″ brush to paint the brownstone highlight and shadow.

- Paint the **Highlight wash** on the top and right of each brownstone block. Paint the **Shadow wash** on the bottom and left of each brownstone block.

Paint the cast shadows.

- The light is coming from the upper right. Paint the shadow cast by the brownstone on the fieldstone. Remember that the shadow line will not be a constant width. The spaces between the stones are deeper, so the shadows in those places will be wider.

- The brownstone will also cast a shadow on the window frame. When painting this cast shadow, keep the bottom edge of the brush parallel with the light direction. This will automatically line up the shadows with the direction of the light. This is especially helpful with irregular items. (See NOTES for Step 7.)

Titles in **bold** indicate paint names found on the elevation.

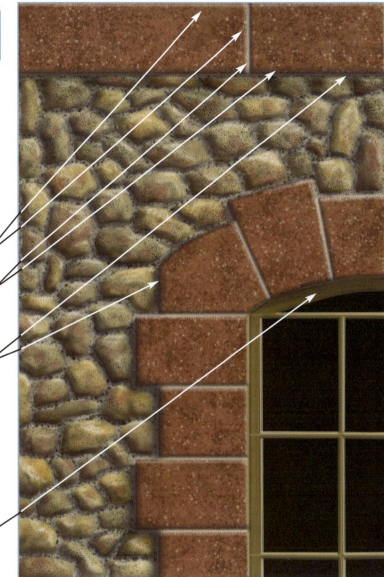

Scale, 2 units wide × 3 units high.

NOTES

- **P.S.** A lamp, curtains, even a person could be in the window.
- This project is fairly complicated. Adding to it might be redundant.
- Consider painting this project in two steps or assignments.
- Consider using this project as a midterm project because of the complexity.

Brick

WORK SURFACE

A 4′ × 6′ traditional or hard-covered flat.

TYPE OF PAINT

Rosco *Off Broadway* paint, Rosco *Iddings Deep Colors*, or a commercial latex substitute. See the COLOR SAMPLES page at the beginning of this book for brand and color suggestions.

TYPES OF CONSISTENCY

OUT OF THE CAN—Rosco suggests that the paint can be used right out of the can. This consistency might be thick. Add water to achieve a NORMAL consistency (see below).

NORMAL—Thick enough just to cover other projects in a single coat, assuming that the difference between the paint colors is not too great.

DILUTED—1 or 2 parts paint to 1 part water added to the NORMAL paint consistency.

WATERY—1 part paint to 5 to 10 parts water added to the NORMAL paint consistency. Rosco says: "Diluting with more than 2 parts water may reduce binder strength. Add Rosco *Clear Acrylic Glaze* to restore adhesion and flexibility."

PAINTING TECHNIQUES

CARTOON—A line drawing of a paint elevation used as a guide for a painting project.

SCUMBLE (paint technique)—Blending two or more random patches of color; the size of the patches and the amount of blend will vary depending on the project.

DRY BRUSH (paint technique)—Dragging a brush loaded with paint across a dry surface (also called "combing").

SPATTER (paint technique)—A method of texture using a brush to throw drops of paint on a surface.

HIGHLIGHT WASH (paint technique)—A light, translucent paint used to represent the reflection of light or an area that receives the greatest amount of illumination.

SHADOW WASH (paint technique)—A dark, transparent paint used to suggest a shadow cast from one object on another.

Glossary

BRICK—A handy-sized unit of building or paving material; typically rectangular and composed of moist clay hardened by heat.

OMNIDIRECTIONAL BRUSH STROKE—Applying paint in a random pattern of brush strokes, usually in a figure-eight configuration. This will leave very little grain in the paint when dry.

MULLION—The large vertical or radiating members that divide units of a window, door, or screen.

MUNTIN—Small horizontal wood strips that separate and hold each pane of glass in a door or window.

CHALK—A stick of soft white or buff limestone composed chiefly of the shells of foraminifers.

KRAFT PAPER—Nonabsorbent paper used to protect against spills and protect scenery from additional paint applications.

MORTAR—A building material; usually a mixture of cement, lime, or gypsum plaster with sand and water that hardens and is used in masonry work to connect bricks or blocks.

Scale, 2 units wide × 3 units high.

TOOLS NEEDED
(See the Project pages for details.)

- **A collection of scene and housepainting brushes**

- **Chalk or charcoal for cartooning**

- **Tape measure**

- **Straightedge or lining stick**

Brick scumble #1 Raw umber	**Brick wash #3** Black - 50% opacity	**Light window trim** Pthalo blue/gray - light
Brick scumble #2 Burnt sienna	**Mortar** Cool gray - medium	**Medium window trim** Pthalo blue/gray - medium
Brick scumble #3 Deep red	**Brick scumble #4** Raw sienna	**Dark window trim** Pthalo blue/gray - dark
Brick wash #1 Raw sienna - 50% opacity	**Shadow wash** Black/violet - 10% opacity	
Brick wash #2 Deep red - 50% opacity	**Hightlight wash** White/pthalo blue - 10% opacity	

10

11

12

13

14

Scale, 2 units wide × 3 units high.

STEP 1
Scumble the Red Brick

Use **Brick scumble #1**, **Brick scumble #2**, and **Brick scumble #3** for the scumble base. (See NOTES.)

- Add a little more water to the NORMAL consistency paint. This will help the blending process.

Use a 2″ or 3″ brush to paint patches of all three scumble colors.

- Work a quarter of the flat at a time.

- The patches of color can touch each other but should not blend at this time. (See the detail toward the bottom of the elevation example.)

- Either use three brushes or clean the brush out a bit after applying each color.

- Before the paint dries, use a clean brush to blend the colors. Use an omnidirectional brush stroke when blending the colors together.

- Don't overwork the blending. The goal is to have a number of colors as a result of the blending. There should be places where the three colors are not blended at all.

Titles in **bold** indicate paint names found on the elevation.

NOTES

- In terms of time, scumble should take only a little longer than base painting. Scumble should be a quick technique, and it adds more interest than one color of base paint.

- Two major factors affect the look of scumble: One is the number and contrast of the paint colors, and the second is the size of the brushes used for the technique.

- Have a bucket of clean water nearby. Although this seems obvious, handy clean water will solve a variety of problems.

STEP 2
Cartoon the Red Brick

Use chalk or vine charcoal to cartoon the red brick. (See NOTES.)

- Please measure very carefully. Take time to avoid mistakes.

- Many projects are less than successful because of mistakes made in measurement.

- The bricks in the bottom seven courses of bricks are 9″ wide by 3″ high.

- The bricks below the window are 3″ wide by 4″ high.

- The remainder of the red bricks are 2″ high and varied lengths.

Titles in **bold** indicate paint names found on the elevation.

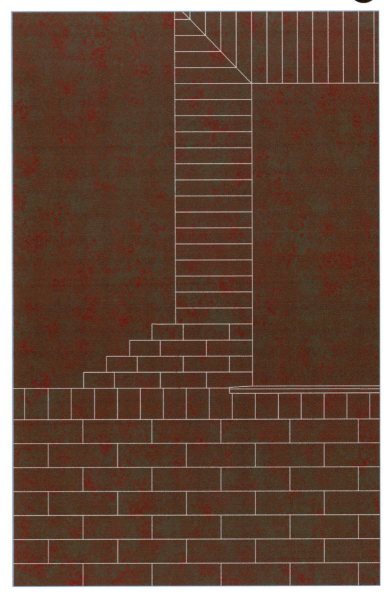

Scale, 2 units wide × 3 units high.

NOTES
- When cartooning a flat, use chalk or other light-color material on dark surfaces.

- When cartooning a flat, use vine charcoal or other dark material on light surfaces.

- Make sure that whatever is used can be removed or covered up when cartoon lines are no longer needed.

- Remember, some materials (such as marker) will not always cover with paint. This might be a problem with the current project and might be a real problem when moving to the next project.

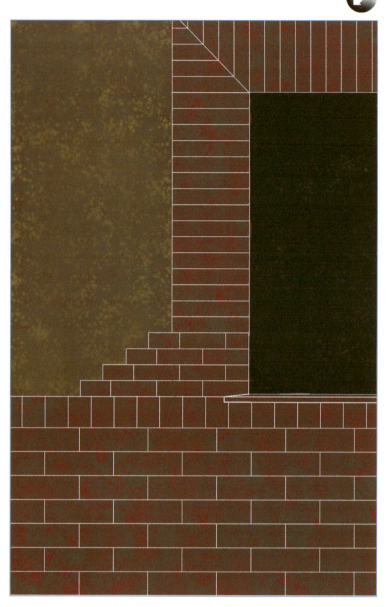

Scale, 2 units wide × 3 units high.

STEP 3
Scumble the Brown Brick and Window Background

Use **Brick scumble #1**, **Brick scumble #2**, and **Brick scumble #4** for the brown brick scumble.

- Add a little more water to the NORMAL consistency paint. This will help the blending process.

Scumble the brown brick using the same technique for the red brick, only with slightly different colors mentioned above.

- Be careful not to slop the paint on the red brick scumble.
- Mask with tape if necessary; however, tape can be very unpredictable and might pull up previously painted work.

Use **Brick wash #3** and the **Dark window trim** to scumble the window background.

- Base paint the entire window area with the **Window scumble**, then scumble in a little of the **Dark window trim**.
- Make sure to paint enough area for the window, almost to the cartoon line.
- It is not necessary to get extremely close to the red brick; the window frame will cover the seam.
- Painting to the edge will help when painting the window later.

Titles in **bold** indicate paint names found on the elevation.

NOTES

- Scene painting brushes are expensive, aren't they? Always leave enough time at the end of a painting session for proper cleanup, especially brush cleanup.

- Don't soak paint brushes. Soaking can cause bristles to droop, ferrules to rust, and handles to swell.

- Use lukewarm water and a mild soap to clean brushes.

- A wire brush can harm the bristles and even pull them out from the ferrule. Use a brush comb specifically intended for fine brushes.

- Place the brush back in its plastic keeper. If the brush did not come in one, use a piece of paper towel to gently wrap the bristles.

Things to Remember

13

Scale, 2 units wide × 3 units high.

STEP 4
Cartoon the Brown Brick and Window

Use chalk or charcoal to cartoon the brown brick.

- Please measure very carefully. Take time to avoid mistakes.
- Many projects are less than successful because of mistakes made in measurement.
- All of the brown bricks are 9″ wide by 3″ high. The small ends are either cut brick by the window or parts of brick not seen.

Use chalk to cartoon the window.

- Please measure very carefully. Take time to avoid mistakes.
- Many projects are less than successful because of mistakes made in measurement.
- The great number of lines can be confusing.
- If the process is too confusing, consider cartooning a few lines (the window frame) and painting that area. Let it dry, then continue with other parts of the window.
- Although this approach will take additional time, it will take less time than making a mistake and having to repaint the entire window.
- Check and double check the cartooning. Have a friend check the layout for confirmation if you are unsure of your measuring.

Titles in **bold** indicate paint names found on the elevation.

NOTES

- Straightedges and lining sticks are painting guides used for painting straight lines.

- These tools can be any size, but the longest length is probably 6′. It is difficult to reach any farther. Sticks used for painting scenery on the floor have longer handles and can be longer in length because reach is not an issue.

- A wooden stick is the most popular material. It must be straight and lightweight. The edges are beveled on the bottom. The bevel keeps the painting edge away from the scenery and the paint will not seep under the stick. Place a handle in the middle of the stick.

- Place a piece of waterproof tape over the edges. When the paint builds up on the edges, remove the tape, replace it, and continue painting.

Things to Remember

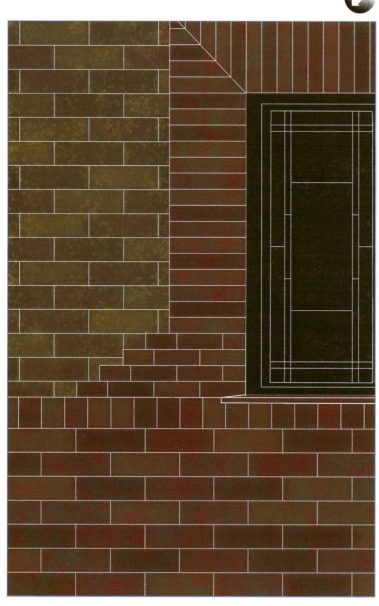

Scale, 2 units wide × 3 units high.

STEP 5
Dry Brush the Brick

Use **Brick wash #1**, **Brick wash #2**, and **Brick wash #3** for the brick dry brush. Keep a close eye on the paint elevation and duplicate the color of the bricks.

- Brushes used for the dry brush technique should be the same width as the brick (2″ or 3″). (See NOTES.)

- Paint the wash without the straightedge, but keep in mind that variations in the dry brush should not be too wild.

- The consistency of the paint should be DILUTED.

- Small variations in the dry brush are desirable.

- Most of the bricks have at least one color of dry brush. Some can have more than one.

Titles in **bold** indicate paint names found on the elevation.

IMPORTANT!

- Check the previous step. This is a subtle paint application of not too much paint. Paint the first few strokes of the dry brush technique on a test flat to ensure applying the correct amount of paint to the full project.

NOTES

- A brand new and well cared for brush is not the best choice for the dry brush technique in this project.

- Please take care of paint brushes. Even with proper care, brushes will age and bristles will begin to separate. Don't throw away these brushes. They will work very well for this type of dry brush, spattering, and other painting techniques.

- Cut into the bristles of a new and inexpensive brush if an old brush is not available. This technique will ruin the brush for other applications.

- Inexpensive, disposable bristled brushes are great tools for painting this type of dry brush technique.

Things to Remember

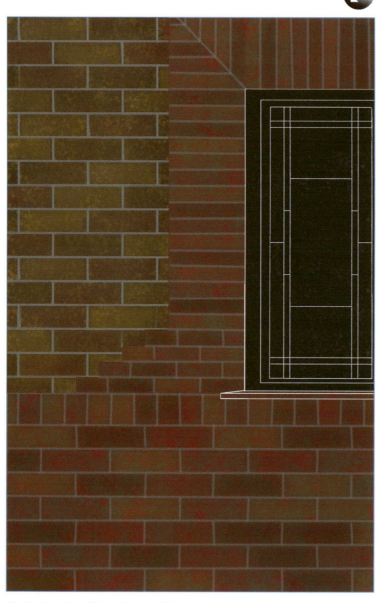

Scale, 2 units wide × 3 units high.

STEP 6
Paint the Mortar

Use the **Mortar** paint color for the mortar.

- The width of the brush is not critical if using the edge of a flat-ferrule brush.

- Substitute a scenic fitch or liner, not more than 1/4″ on a side; however, a brush this small will not hold a great deal of paint. This will be a problem when painting longer lines.

- The lines should be straight, but the pressure can be variable.

- Use a straightedge. (See NOTES.)

Titles in **bold** indicate paint names found on the elevation.

NOTES

- Always use a straightedge for painting straight lines.

- "I can paint a straight line without a straightedge" or "It takes too long to paint and move a straightedge" or "It looks just fine without using a straightedge" are just a few of the excuses for not using a straightedge that are heard on a regular basis. All of these excuses are invalid!

- Mortar lines *must be straight and must line up vertically*. Masons are precise.

STEP 7
Spatter the Flat

Use **Brick wash #1**, **Brick wash #2**, and **Brick wash #3**.

- The consistency is important. Proper consistency will help the spatter process. (See NOTES.)

Use a 3″ or 4″ brush to paint the spatter. This is a good time to use an old brush that might not be good for anything else.

- Start painting with **Brick wash #1**.
- Dip the brush in the paint and use the side of the bucket to remove excess paint from the brush, then swipe the brush on the floor or other approved area to remove even more excess.
- It doesn't matter where the spatter starts for this project.
- The spatter in this project should be more or less even.
- Repeat the process with **Brick wash #2** and **Brick wash #3**.

Titles in **bold** indicate paint names found on the elevation.

Scale, 2 units wide × 3 units high.

IMPORTANT!

- Cover the window with Kraft paper before spattering the flat. The other option would be to postpone painting the window entirely until after the spatter in this step is applied.

NOTES

- The consistency of the spatter paint should be DILUTED. If the paint is too thick, it will stay on the brush. If the paint is too thin, it will not read very well on the finished flat.

- There are many ways of applying spatter. One method is to hit the spatter brush against a stick or hand to control the application. Flicking the wrist in the direction of the painting surface but avoiding back-snap is another possibility. Wildly swinging the brush is likely to deposit paint on all adjacent surfaces, including coworkers. This will make the supervisors upset.

- This is a small area to spatter. A sprayer can be used for larger projects.

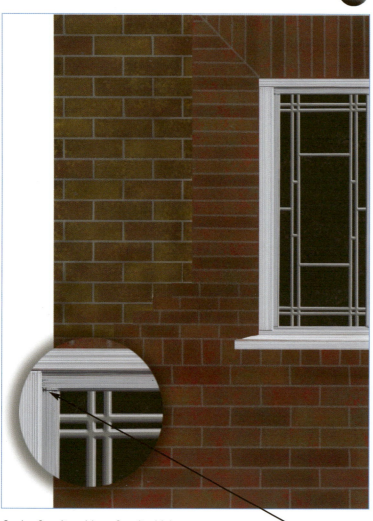

Scale, 2 units wide × 3 units high.

STEP 8
Paint the Window

Use the **Light window trim**, **Medium window trim**, and **Dark window trim** to paint the window. (See NOTES.)

- Start with the leading on the window. Paint over the chalk lines with the **Medium window trim**.

- Now paint the sides of the leading that are toward the light with the **Light window trim** paint color (the right and top of the leading).

- Now paint the sides of the leading that are away from the light with the **Dark window trim** color (the left and bottom of the leading). (See the detail in the elevation example.)

Finish the remainder of the window frame.

- Base paint the inner and outer window frames with **Dark window trim.**

- Use the **Medium window trim** paint and the **Light window trim** paint for both the inner and outer window frames. Use a dry brush technique. This will appear as wood grain on the painted window trim.

- The outer window frame should receive a little extra dry brush with the **Light window trim** paint.

- Add cut lines at the joints between two pieces of window frame. Remember to keep these lines subtle.

Titles in **bold** indicate paint names found on the elevation.

NOTES

- When painting trim elements, it is often a good idea to work from farther to closer. Begin with the objects that appear to be the farthest back. The paint applied will cover the edges from previous painting.

- The **Dark window trim** and **Light window trim** lines are thin. Don't completely cover the **Medium window trim** lines when adding the light and dark colors. All the leading on the windows should have all three colors.

STEP 9
Shadow

Use the **Shadow wash** for the brick cast shadow. The consistency of the paint should be WATERY.

Please test the paint. (See NOTES.)
Paint the cast shadows.
The two window frames will cast shadows:

- The outer window frame will cast shadows.

- The inner window frame will cast a shadow on the window and the leading; however, that shadow will only be noticeable on the leading.

- The red brick will cast a shadow on the brown brick because the brown brick is recessed.

- The window sill will cast a shadow.

- This course of red brick will cast a shadow on the recessed brick below.

- Place small shadow lines to help separate the brick.

Paint the red bricks with shadow.

- Use the **Shadow wash** to paint the two sides of the brick away from the light (the left side and the bottom). A little of the shadow should overlap the brick.

- Use the same technique to paint the brown bricks.

Titles in **bold** indicate paint names found on the elevation.

Scale, 2 units wide × 3 units high.

NOTES

- Practice mixing and using shadow and highlight washes. It is important to master this skill. Highlight and shadow washes are used for every project. It will take practice.

- Please test all paints, especially washes. Darker washes will tend to dry with less intensity and lighter washes will tend to dry with more intensity (but it is very unpredictable).

- Stir this paint on a regular basis. The pigment will settle more than paint of regular consistency.

- A small flat (maybe 2′ × 3′) will work well as a test flat.

- The **Shadow wash** should be half on and half off the edge of the brick. The shadow half on the brick will read as a thickness, and the shadow half off the brick will read as the cast shadow.

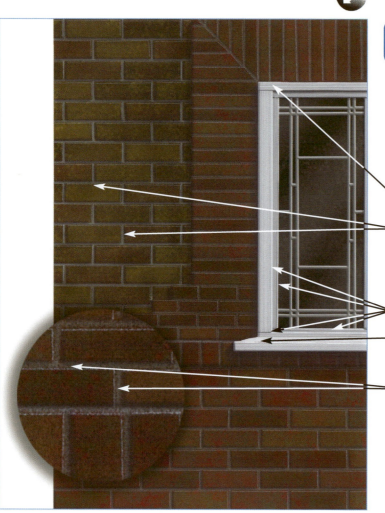

Scale, 2 units wide × 3 units high.

STEP 10
Highlight

Use the **Highlight wash** for painting highlights. The consistency of the paint should be WATERY.

- Please test the paint.

Paint the highlights.

- Give the top edge of the window frame a sharp highlight.

- Use the **Highlight wash** to paint the brown brick edges that are toward the light, the right side, and the top. The highlight is the illumination of the edge of the brick and is very thin.

- Highlight edges of the window frame.

- Give the top of the window sill extra light.

- Use the highlight to paint the red brick edges that are toward the light, the right side, and the top; the highlight is the illumination of the edge of the brick and is very thin.

Use the **Highlight wash** to spatter a reflection in the window.

- This is a very subtle paint technique. It is better to omit this application than to apply an excessive amount of paint.

- Consider adding a small amount of additional water to the wash.

- Please test the paint.

Titles in **bold** indicate paint names found on the elevation.

NOTES

- Painting vertically, painting up, or the Eastern style:

  - The work is attached to a moving frame that travels up and down.

  - Alternatively, the work can be attached to a fixed frame, and using some sort of scaffolding the painter moves up and down.

  - Wet paint and washes will run and are a challenge to control. It's that gravity thing.

- Painting on the floor, or the Continental style:

  - Be careful not to kick over paint or walk on wet paint areas.

  - Brush extensions made from bamboo or plastic are necessary to avoid backaches.

  - Plenty of space is necessary.

13

Things to Remember _____

PROJECT 14

Clapboard Wall, Door, and Shutter

WORK SURFACE

A 4′ × 6′ traditional or hard-covered flat.

TYPE OF PAINT

Rosco *Off Broadway* paint, Rosco *Iddings Deep Colors*, or a commercial latex substitute. See the COLOR SAMPLES page at the beginning of this book for brand and color suggestions.

TYPES OF CONSISTENCY

OUT OF THE CAN—Rosco suggests that the paint can be used right out of the can. This consistency might be thick. Add water to achieve a NORMAL consistency (see below).

NORMAL—Thick enough just to cover other projects in a single coat, assuming that the difference between the paint colors is not too great.

DILUTED—1 or 2 parts paint to 1 part water added to the NORMAL paint consistency.

WATERY—1 part paint to 5 to 10 parts water added to the NORMAL paint consistency. Rosco says: "Diluting with more than 2 parts water may reduce binder strength. Add Rosco *Clear Acrylic Glaze* to restore adhesion and flexibility."

PAINTING TECHNIQUES

BASE PAINT (paint technique)—The first paint color or colors used in a specific painting project, usually the predominant color.

CARTOON—A line drawing of a paint elevation used as a guide for a painting project.

DRY BRUSH (paint technique)—Dragging a brush loaded with paint across a dry surface (also called "combing").

SHADOW WASH (paint technique)—A dark, transparent paint used to suggest a shadow cast from one object on another.

HIGHLIGHT WASH (paint technique)—A light, translucent paint used to represent the reflection of light or an area that receives the greatest amount of illumination.

DISTRESSING—Deliberately marring to give an effect of age.

Glossary

CLAPBOARD—A narrow board usually thicker at one edge than the other; used for the siding of a building.

SHUTTERS—A usually movable cover or screen for a window or door.

MULLION—The large vertical or radiating members that divide units of a window, door, or screen.

MUNTIN—Small horizontal wood strips that separate and hold each pane of glass in a door or window.

CHALK—A stick of soft white or buff limestone composed chiefly of the shells of foraminifers.

CUTLINE (paint technique)—Small detail lines that help to differentiate edges and planes.

PAINT ELEVATION—A scaled, color drawing or painting of a piece of scenery provided by the scenic designer.

STRAIGHT-EDGE—A straight length of wood with a handle that ensures the painting of a straight line.

Scale, 2 units wide × 3 units high.

TOOLS NEEDED
(See the Project pages for details.)

- A collection of scene and housepainting brushes

- Chalk or charcoal for cartooning

- Tape measure

- Straightedge or lining stick

Base Raw umber - light	**Window scumble** Ultramarine blue	**Shadow wash** Black/violet - 10% opacity
Clapboards and trim White	**Shutter** Chrome oxide green - med.	**Distressed wash** Burnt umber
Window background Black	**Hightlight wash** White/blue - 10% opacity	**Shutter highlight** Chrome oxide green - light

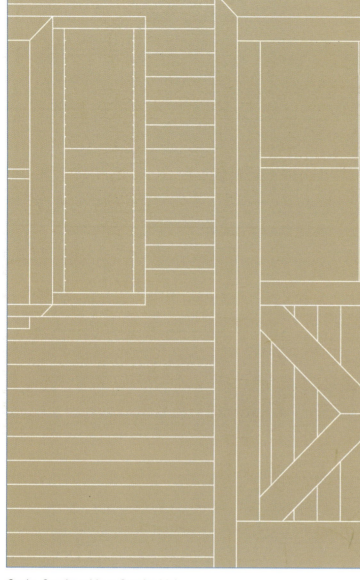

Scale, 2 units wide × 3 units high.

STEP 1
Base Paint and Cartoon the Flat

Base paint the flat with the **Base** color.

- If this flat is used for a scene painting class, the paint should be just thick enough to cover the previous painting project.

- If this is a new flat, the paint should be just thick enough to cover the flat.

- In either case, remember that a lot of additional paint will go on this flat. Use only enough paint to cover the flat.

- Let the flat dry completely.

Use chalk or charcoal to cartoon the planks.

- Please measure very carefully. Many projects are ruined because of mistakes made in measurement.

- Use a straightedge or chalk line the straight lines. (See NOTES.)

Titles in **bold** indicate paint names found on the elevation.

NOTES

- When cartooning a flat, use chalk or other light-color material on dark surfaces.

- When cartooning a flat, use vine charcoal or other dark material on light surfaces.

- Make sure that whatever is used can be removed or covered up when the cartoon lines are no longer needed.

- Remember, some materials (such as marker) will not always cover with paint. This might be a problem with the current project and might be a real problem when moving to the next project.

STEP 2
Dry Brush the Clapboards

Use a 3″ brush to paint the **Clapboards** and **trim**.

- The consistency of the paint should have a little more water than NORMAL.

- Load the brush with a minimum of paint. Lightly press and move the brush over the flat. The **Base** should not completely cover.

- Go as long as possible before lifting the brush or running out of paint. If the brush runs out of paint, lift it gradually so as to prevent a visible brush line.

- Variation in the dry brush is desirable. Roll the brush when painting a plank or rotate the brush from side to side while keeping the bristles flat on the surface. Either method will achieve variation in the brush stroke.

Titles in **bold** indicate paint names found on the elevation.

Scale, 2 units wide × 3 units high.

14

NOTES

- A brand new and well cared for brush is not the best choice for the dry brush technique in this project.

- Please take care of paint brushes. Even with proper care, brushes will age and bristles will begin to separate. Don't throw away these brushes. They will work very well for this type of dry brush, spattering, and other painting techniques.

- Cut into the bristles of a new and inexpensive brush if an old brush is not available. This technique will ruin the brush for other applications.

- Inexpensive, disposable bristled brushes are great tools for painting this type of dry brush technique.

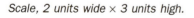

Scale, 2 units wide × 3 units high.

STEP 3
Window Base and Scumble

Mix the **Window background** and **Window scumble** paint colors used for the scumble.

- The consistency should have a little more water than NORMAL.

Use a 2″ or 3″ brush to paint the window area.

- Base paint the window area with the **Window background**.
- While the base is still wet, blend in a small amount of the **Window scumble**.
- Work quickly.
- Don't overwork the blending.

It is important to apply paint techniques all the way to the edges. The dry brush should not stop before the trim, and the scumble should cover the entire area.

- One method of achieving this goal is to paint over the cartoon lines. (See the example on the previous page.) When the dry brush is no longer wet, cartoon and base the area again.
- The window frame is also re-based after the scumble has dried.
- The alternative to this procedure is to mask the areas not to be painted with Kraft paper or tape.

Titles in **bold** indicate paint names found on the elevation.

NOTES
- In terms of time, scumble should take only a little longer than base painting. Scumble should be a quick technique, and it adds more interest than one color of base paint.

- Two major factors affect the look of scumble: One is the number and contrast of the paint colors, and the second is the size of the brushes used for the technique.

- Have a bucket of clean water nearby. Although this seems obvious, handy clean water will solve a variety of problems.

STEP 4
Dry Brush the Window and Door Frame

Use a 2″ and 3″ brush to paint the **Clapboards** and **trim**.

- The consistency of the paint should have a little more water than NORMAL.

- Load the brush with a minimum of paint. Lightly press and move the brush over the flat. The **Base** should not completely cover.

- Go as long as possible before lifting the brush or running out of paint. If the brush runs out of paint, lift it gradually so as to prevent a visible brush line.

- Variation in the dry brush is desirable. Roll the brush when painting a plank or rotate the brush from side to side while keeping the bristles flat on the surface. Either method will achieve variation in the brush stroke.

Paint the items that appear to be in the back and work forward. The paint applied will cover the edges from previous painting. On the door:

- Paint the "X" on the bottom of the door and the window mullions.

- Now paint the toggle. This painting will cover those edges.

- Next, paint the stile, which will cover the toggle and trim edges.

- Paint the rails last. They will cover the remainder of the edges.

Titles in **bold** indicate paint names found on the elevation.

Scale, 2 units wide × 3 units high.

NOTES

- A wood-grain "rocker" tool can be another method of painting wood grain.

- Plastic wood-grain "rocker" tools are popular and can be purchased at most hardware and home improvement stores. A light base is applied and allowed to dry. A darker and more diluted paint is applied on top. A coarse grain is achieved by dragging the tool and simultaneously rocking the tool up and down. It is interesting, even fascinating, the way this tool works.

- The plastic wood-graining tool does have its limitations. The results can lack a certain degree of sophistication without additional painting. Ideally, a smooth, hard surface is required. Sizes can limit effective application.

Things to Remember

STEP 5
Shutter Dry Brush and Detail Lines

Use a 1-1/2″ brush to paint the **Shutter**.

- The consistency of the paint should have a little more water than NORMAL.

- Load the brush with a minimum of paint. Lightly press and move the brush over the flat. The **Base** should not completely cover.

- Go as long as possible before lifting the brush or running out of paint. If the brush runs out of paint, lift it gradually so as to prevent a visible brush line.

- Variation in the dry brush is desirable.

Paint the items that appear to be in the back and work forward. The new paint will cover the edges from previous painting. On the shutter:

- Paint the horizontal slats and the middle toggle.

- Now paint the stiles on the sides. This painting will cover the edges of the slats.

- Paint the rails on the top and bottom last. They will cover the ends of the stiles.

Use **Shadow wash** and a small brush to add detail lines to the ends of boards on the door, door frame, and window frame.

Titles in **bold** indicate paint names found on the elevation.

Scale, 2 units wide × 3 units high.

14

NOTES

- It is amazing how average the painting looks at this stage.

- It seems a significant amount of work for little payback.

- Have faith in the painting. Shadow and highlight will add the finishing touch.

- Not painting all the way to the edges of a designated paint area is a common problem with beginning painters. Techniques should cover the extent of the designated painting area.

- Make sure that all techniques are complete. Spatter, dry brush, splatter, etc., all must go to the edges of the flat or area.

- Failure to do so will be detrimental to the look of the finished painting.

Things to Remember

STEP 6
Shadow

Look at the example.

Use the **Shadow wash** to paint the shadows:

- A shadow on the edge of the window frame to suggest a bevel
- A shadow on the edge of the door and window frame to suggest a bevel
- A cast shadow because the mullions are recessed
- A cast shadow (See NOTES.)
- A cast shadow
- A small shadow caused by a gap between the shutter and the window frame
- A cast shadow
- A cast shadow
- A cast shadow
- A cast shadow
- A cast shadow

Notice that a few of the chalk cartoon lines still show at this stage of the painting.

Titles in **bold** indicate paint names found on the elevation.

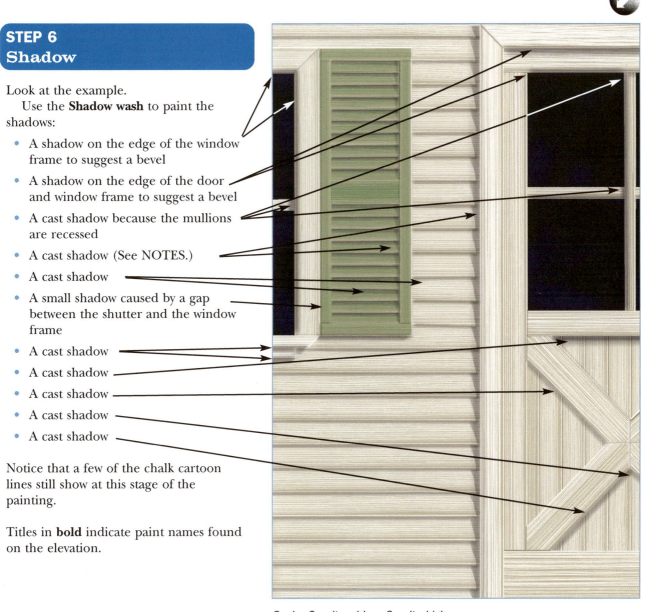

Scale, 2 units wide × 3 units high.

NOTES
- The clapboards are attached to the wall on an angle.
- As a result, the top of the clapboard is farther away from the door frame.
- The cast shadow from the door frame will hit the bottom of the clapboard before it hits the top of the clapboard; therefore, the shadow on the clapboard is wider at the top.
- The same is true for the interior of the shutters.

STEP 7
Highlight

Look at the example.
Use the **Highlight wash** to paint these highlights:

- A thin line on the top of the frame

Use the **Shutter wash** to paint these highlights:

- A thin line on the edges facing the light
- A very thin line on the edges of the shutter slats

Use the **Highlight wash** to paint these highlights:.

- A thin line on the frame edges facing the light

Use the **Shutter wash** to paint these highlights:

- A thin line on the edges facing the light

Use the **Highlight wash** to paint these highlights:

- A thin line on the edges facing the light

Titles in **bold** indicate paint names found on the elevation.

Scale, 2 units wide × 3 units high.

NOTES

- Practice mixing and using shadow and highlight washes. It is important to master this skill. Highlight and shadow washes are used for every project. It will take practice.

- Please test all paints, especially washes. Darker washes will tend to dry with less intensity and lighter washes will tend to dry with more intensity (but it is very unpredictable).

- Stir this paint on a regular basis. The pigment will settle more than paint of regular consistency.

- A small flat (maybe 2′ × 3′) will work well as a test flat.

- The shadow wash should be half on and half off the edge of the brick. The shadow half on the brick will read as a thickness, and the shadow half off the brick will read as the cast shadow.

STEP 8
Final Distressing

Splatter the wainscot for a distressed look.

- The wall and the wainscot should have the same dirty look.

- Mix **Wash #1** with additional water. Use this paint to splatter the flat. Use less paint with more water for splattering. (See NOTES.)

- The effect of splatter in this project will add age and dirt to the wall. The goal is to apply the splatter in an uneven pattern.

- Either splatter the paint directly on the flat or splatter clear water on the flat before the paint splatter is applied.

- Splatter paint with little pigment might not require the water application before the splatter is applied. Please test the mixing and application of splatter. Allow to dry for a true test.

- Repeat the technique with **Wash #2**.

Titles in **bold** indicate paint names found on the elevation.

Scale, 2 units wide × 3 units high.

NOTES

- Have a bucket of clean water handy when splattering. If the splatter wash is too heavy and defined, splatter clean water to help diffuse and blend the paint.

- **P.S.** There is no end to the amount of dirt, filth, and degradation that could be added to the flat.

- Consider adding additional distressing.

- Try adding foliage; for example, vines could grow up the wall or plants might grow in front of the wall.

- A barrel or part of a barrel could stand in front of the house. Shovels, hoes, or rakes might lean against the wall.

PROJECT 15

Ornament

WORK SURFACE

A 4′ × 6′ traditional or hard-covered flat.

TYPE OF PAINT

Rosco *Off Broadway* paint, Rosco *Iddings Deep Colors*, or a commercial latex substitute. See the COLOR SAMPLES page at the beginning of this book for brand and color suggestions.

TYPES OF CONSISTENCY

OUT OF THE CAN—Rosco suggests that the paint can be used right out of the can. This consistency might be thick. Add water to achieve a NORMAL consistency (see below).

NORMAL—Thick enough just to cover other projects in a single coat, assuming that the difference between the paint colors is not too great.

DILUTED—1 or 2 parts paint to 1 part water added to the NORMAL paint consistency.

WATERY—1 part paint to 5 to 10 parts water added to the NORMAL paint consistency. Rosco says: "Diluting with more than 2 parts water may reduce binder strength. Add Rosco *Clear Acrylic Glaze* to restore adhesion and flexibility."

PAINTING TECHNIQUES

GRADED WET BLEND (paint technique)—Arranged in a scale or series; a smooth blend of colors using a gradation, usually a linear pattern blended together (sometimes called "gradient").

BASE PAINT (paint technique)—The first paint color or colors used in a specific painting project, usually the predominant color.

CARTOON—A line drawing of a paint elevation used as a guide for a painting project.

MARBLE (paint technique)—The application of paint in a layer or layers to duplicate the look of marble.

SHADOW WASH (paint technique)—A dark, transparent paint used to suggest a shadow cast from one object on another.

HIGHLIGHT WASH (paint technique)—A light, translucent paint used to represent the reflection of light or an area that receives the greatest amount of illumination.

Glossary

GRADIENT—The rate of graded ascent or descent.

MARBLE—Limestone that is more or less crystallized by metamorphism; varieties of marble range from granular to compact in texture and are capable of taking a high polish.

GRAIN (in marble)—Stratification of the partials in a piece of marble.

ORNAMENT—Something that lends grace or beauty.

HIGHLIGHT—The application of a higher value of color in an attempt to create the illusion of dimension.

HOLIDAY—Part of a surface unintentionally left unpainted.

PAINT ELEVATION—A scaled, color drawing or painting of a piece of scenery provided by the scenic designer.

STRAIGHTEDGE—A straight length of wood with a handle that ensures the painting of a straight line.

Scale, 2 units wide × 3 units high.

LIGHT DIRECTION

TOOLS NEEDED
(See the Project pages for details.)

- A collection of scene and housepainting brushes

- Chalk or charcoal for cartooning

- Tape measure

- Straightedge or lining stick

- A feather for marble grain

 Gradient #1
Black

 Gradient #2
Burnt umber

 Gradient #3
Burnt sienna

 Ornament dark #3
Burnt umber/black

 Ornament dark #2
Burnt umber

 **Ornament dark #1**
Burnt sienna

 **Ornament base**
Raw sienna

 **Ornament light #1**
Yellow ochre

 **Ornament light #2**
Lemon yellow

 **Outer panel wash**
Raw sienna/white - 10% opacity

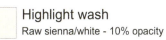 **Highlight wash**
Raw sienna/white - 10% opacity

 Shadow wash
Black/violet - 10% opacity

 **Inner panel wash**
Burnt umber - 5% opacity

Paint in this area
GRADIENT #1

Paint in this area
A blend of **GRADIENT #1** and **GRADIENT #2**

Paint in this area
GRADIENT #2

Paint in this area
A blend of **GRADIENT #2** and **GRADIENT #3**

Paint in this area
GRADIENT #3

Scale, 2 units wide × 3 units high.

15

STEP 1
Gradient Background

Prepare the paint used for the graded wet blend (**Gradient #1**, **Gradient #2**, and **Gradient #3**).

- These paints should be NORMAL consistency. Mix enough paint for this step. The sum of the three colors combined should only be a little more than the quantity needed to base the entire flat. (See NOTES.)

The purpose of the graded wet blend is to achieve an even progression from one color to another.

- Divide the flat into three horizontal sections.
- The bottom section is the largest.
- Base the top section with **Gradient #1**.
- Base the middle section with **Gradient #2**. These paints should almost meet in the blended area.

Now blend these two colors before the paint has a chance to dry.

- Use a clean, damp brush for the blending.
- Work quickly and use a light stroke.
- Don't overwork this technique.

Repeat this procedure with the next two areas and use **Gradient #2** and **Gradient #3**. (See NOTES.)

Titles in **bold** indicate paint names found on the elevation.

NOTES

- When these three paints are correctly mixed, place a drop of one color into the other buckets. This will give a visual clue if the paint is mixed properly. A small drop of the other colors won't affect the paint.

- If **Gradient #2** is dry when beginning to blend **Gradients #2** and **#3**, consider re-basing the bottom of the second section with **Gradient #2**.

- A graded wet blend can be a difficult technique to master.

STEP 2
Base Paint and Cartoon the Flat

Cartoon the area that will be the ornament.

- Use chalk or charcoal to cartoon the flat. (See NOTES.)

- Please measure very carefully. Many projects are ruined because of mistakes made in measurement.

- There are many ways to approach cartooning a flat. Using a grid for this project might be a good idea. (See NOTES.)

- Check Steps 2 and 3 of Project 6 for additional details.

Base paint the flat with the **Ornament base**.

- The paint should be just thick enough to cover the previous painting project on a used flat.

- Dip the brush in a small amount of paint. Remember to use the tips of the brush.

- Use an omnidirectional brush stroke when base painting.

- Avoid holidays.

Titles in **bold** indicate paint names found on the elevation.

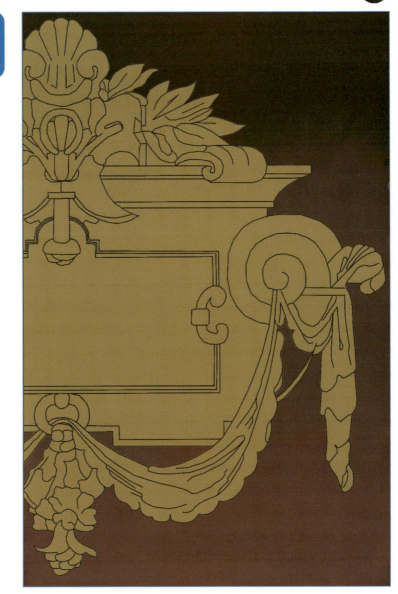

Scale, 2 units wide × 3 units high.

15

IMPORTANT!
- Consider locating the outline of the ornament and then base painting that area. Cartoon the remainder of the ornament area after the base is completely dry.

NOTES

- A grid will be a useful method for cartooning when the shapes drawn are natural and nonarchitectural.

- A grid composed of 1′ squares is small but will work well for this project. A bigger grid should be constructed on larger projects, such as a full drop.

- The blue or red chalk found in most shop snap lines will be difficult to remove from the flat. A new snap line filled with charcoal power would be a great addition to scene painting equipment.

- Consider labeling the grid lines when working with a large project.

Things to Remember

STEP 3
Marble

Base the background for the marble with **Highlight wash** before the extra water is added. Allow to dry.

Splatter or spray a thin layer of clear water on the marble base.

- Add more water to **Gradient #3.** Use the side of the brush and a light amount of pressure to add color to the marble base. This is a quick and loose technique.

Repeat this process with **Ornament base**, **Gradient #2**, and **Gradient #1**.

- Very little paint is needed. First experiment on the test flat.
- Vary the brush stroke when painting these colors. A very wet spatter will be appropriate in a few areas.

Apply more water.

- Immediately splatter or spray a small amount of water over the area. The paint should blend. (See NOTES.)
- Use a clean brush or a damp sponge to help control the water and help the blending process.

Add veins as detail.

- The veins are subtle in this project. Use **Gradient #1** with additional water for this application. (See NOTES.)

Titles in **bold** indicate paint names found on the elevation.

Scale, 2 units wide × 3 units high.

15

> **NOTES**
>
> - The grain of the marble is random and should not have a repetitive pattern. Be aware of the painting and avoid repetition of pattern. This will be more difficult to do the larger the painted area becomes.
>
> - Water will blend the paints, but it is also unpredictable and potentially difficult to control.
>
> - When using a traditional muslin-covered flat, the paint and water might look for the lowest part of the flat, and the result could be a mud puddle.
>
> - Using a feather is slow and tedious but it works well for veining in this project because of the small amount of marble. The side of a thin brush and a little practice will work for larger projects. A flogger used for painting and not for dusting is a fine tool for adding veins to bigger projects.

Things to Remember

STEP 4
Adding Shade

Shade is the part of the object not facing the light. Use **Ornament dark #1** and **Ornament dark #2** to begin adding dimension to the painting.

- It is important to fully appreciate the direction of the light source. (See NOTES.)

- Begin with **Ornament dark #2** and a variety of brushes. The paint should be of the DILUTED consistency.

- Find the surfaces of the ornament not facing the light. Keep the bottom edge of the brush parallel with the light direction when painting. This will automatically line up the shade with the direction of the light.

- Paint the areas of shade. These areas are of different sizes. Change the width of brushes to accommodate the varying sizes of the painting area but always keep the bottom edge of the brush parallel with the light direction.

- Use a straightedge when appropriate.

Use **Ornament dark #1** for the next process.

- Repeat the technique outlined above.

- Paint areas between **Ornament dark #2** and the **Ornament base.** Blending from dark to medium is the goal of this step.

- Keep a bucket of clear water handy to help with the blending process.

Titles in **bold** indicate paint names found on the elevation.

Scale, 2 units wide × 3 units high.

NOTES

- The direction of light is important in scenic painting. Painting shadow wash/cast shadows and highlight wash/reflected highlights is the major way to fool the eye. Notice what a difference the shadow and highlight steps make at the end of a project.

- A clear understanding of light direction and an understanding of the three-dimensional construction of an ornament is absolutely necessary.

- Architectural and geometric objects are predictable in their relationship to light. The irregular curves and surfaces typical of ornaments are less predictable.

Scale, 2 units wide × 3 units high.

STEP 5
Adding Lowlight

Lowlight is a degree down in value from the shade. Use **Ornament dark #3** to add dimension to the painting.

- It is important to fully appreciate the direction of the light source.

- Begin with **Ornament dark #3** and a variety of brushes. The paint should be of the DILUTED consistency. Find the surfaces of the ornament not facing the light. Keep the bottom edge of the brush parallel with the light direction when painting. This will automatically line up the shade with the direction of the light.

- Paint the darkest areas of shade. Not all areas will get **Ornament dark #3**. Save this color for the areas getting the least amount of light. Change the width of brushes to accommodate the varying sizes of the painting area but always keep the bottom edge of the brush parallel with the light direction.

- Use a straightedge when appropriate.

- Keep a bucket of clear water handy to help with the blending process.

Titles in **bold** indicate paint names found on the elevation.

NOTES

- Finding adequate work space is important. Even when space is at a premium, adequate work and storage space is essential.

- Find or build shelves for storing paint cans. Paint cans not properly stored and sealed will dry out or, worse, get kicked over.

- Brushes must be thoroughly cleaned and stored hanging up or flat on an open rack. Old and worn brushes can still be used for certain paint applications. Brushes with gobs of dried paint in them are no longer useful.

- Pride in equipment and environment will lead to pride in the work.

STEP 6
Add Light Tones

Use **Ornament light #1** and **Ornament light #2.**

- Begin with **Ornament light #2** and a variety of brushes. The paint should be of the DILUTED consistency.

- Find the surfaces of the ornament facing the light. Keep the bottom edge of the brush parallel with the light direction when painting. This will automatically line up the painting with the direction of the light.

- Paint the areas of light tones. These areas are of different sizes. Change the width of brushes to accommodate the varying sizes of the painting area but always keep the bottom edge of the brush parallel with the light direction.

- Use a straightedge when appropriate.

Use **Ornament light #1** for the next process.

- Repeat the technique outlined above.

- Paint areas between **Ornament light #2** and the **Ornament base.** Blending from light to medium is the goal of this step.

This procedure is basically Step 3 in reverse. Paint the lightest areas and blend to the shade.

Titles in **bold** indicate paint names found on the elevation.

Scale, 2 units wide × 3 units high.

NOTES

- This project is painted in a *trompe l'oeil* painting style.

- *Trompe l'oeil* is French for "to fool (or deceive) the eye."

- *Trompe l'oeil* techniques were developed in Italy during the Rococo period.

- Painting with perspective and foreshortening plus highlight and shadow are typical of the *trompe l'oeil* style.

- The goal is for audience members to believe that they are seeing objects in three dimensions when they are viewing a two-dimensional surface.

Scale, 2 units wide × 3 units high.

STEP 7
Shadow and Washes on the Center Panels

Prepare the washes used for this step.

- The consistency of the paint should be WATERY.
- Consider adding additional binder.

Use a variety of brushes to paint the cast shadow.

- Paint the cast shadow from the ornament on the gradient and from each element to the adjoining area. (See NOTES.)
- Paint the inner panel with the **Inner panel wash** and the outer panel with the **Outer panel wash**. Both washes have a lot of water, and this application is subtle. This will make the center panel recede.

Use the **Highlight wash** for painting highlights.

- The consistency of the paint should be WATERY.
- Please test the paint.

Paint a few highlights:

- The sharp edges of the cornice trim
- A few of the brightest areas of the ornament

Only a few very bright highlights are added.

Titles in **bold** indicate paint names found on the elevation.

NOTES

- Stir this paint on a regular basis. The pigment will settle more than paint of regular consistency.

- A small flat (maybe 2′ × 3′) will work well as a test flat.

- When painting cast shadows, keep the bottom edge of the brush parallel with the light direction. This will automatically line up the shadows with the direction of the light.

- **P.S.** This is a bit difficult for this project. It is very complete, so what might be added to this project? Try using highlight and shadow to add chiseled writing in the marble or add more detail in the ornament.

Things to Remember

WORK SURFACE

A 4′ × 6′ traditional or hard-covered flat.

TYPE OF PAINT

Rosco *Off Broadway* paint, Rosco *Iddings Deep Colors*, or a commercial latex substitute. See the COLOR SAMPLES page at the beginning of this book for brand and color suggestions.

TYPES OF CONSISTENCY

OUT OF THE CAN—Rosco suggests that the paint can be used right out of the can. This consistency might be thick. Add water to achieve a NORMAL consistency (see below).

NORMAL—Thick enough just to cover other projects in a single coat, assuming that the difference between the paint colors is not too great.

DILUTED—1 or 2 parts paint to 1 part water added to the NORMAL paint consistency.

WATERY—1 part paint to 5 to 10 parts water added to the NORMAL paint consistency. Rosco says: "Diluting with more than 2 parts water may reduce binder strength. Add Rosco *Clear Acrylic Glaze* to restore adhesion and flexibility."

PAINTING TECHNIQUES

BASE PAINT (paint technique)—The first paint color or colors used in a specific painting project, usually the predominant color.

SPATTER (paint technique)—A method of texture using a brush to throw drops of paint on a surface.

CARTOON—A line drawing of a paint elevation used as a guide for a painting project.

STENCILING—Applying paint through holes cut in a sheet of paper or plastic, for example, to create a repetitive pattern.

STAMP—A tool for applying paint made from foam rubber cut in a pattern and fastened to a solid piece of lauan, plywood, or Masonite® (hardboard).

SHADOW WASH (paint technique)—A dark, transparent paint used to suggest a shadow cast from one object on another.

HIGHLIGHT WASH (paint technique)—A light, translucent paint used to represent the reflection of light or an area that receives the greatest amount of illumination.

Glossary

ACETATE (CELLULOSE)—Any of several compounds insoluble in water and used for making textile fibers, packaging sheets, transparent films, and varnishes.

BASEBOARD—Molding attached to the bottom of a wall covering the joint of a wall and the adjoining floor.

KRAFT PAPER—Nonabsorbent paper used to protect against spills and protect scenery from additional paint applications.

GRID—A collection of lines and squares at a reduced scale on a paint elevation and in full scale on a drop or flat; used to transfer a cartoon.

STRAIGHTEDGE—A straight length of wood with a handle that ensures the painting of a straight line.

Scale, 2 units wide × 3 units high.

LIGHT DIRECTION

TOOLS NEEDED
(See the Project pages for details.)

- **A collection of scene and housepainting brushes**

- **Chalk or charcoal for cartooning**

- **Tape measure**

- **Straightedge or lining stick**

- **Materials for stencils and stamps**

Base	Spatter #4	Wallpaper green
Raw umber - light	White/raw umber	Chrome oxide green - medium
Spatter #1	**Wallpaper blue**	**Shadow wash**
Pthalo blue - medium	Pthalo blue - medium	Black/violet - 10% opacity
Spatter #2	**Wallpaper red**	**Cast shadow**
Deep red - medium	Deep red - medium	Raw umber - 10% opacity
Spatter #3	**Wallpaper rust**	**Highlight wash**
Burnt sienna - medium	Burnt sienna - medium	White/raw umber - 10% opacity

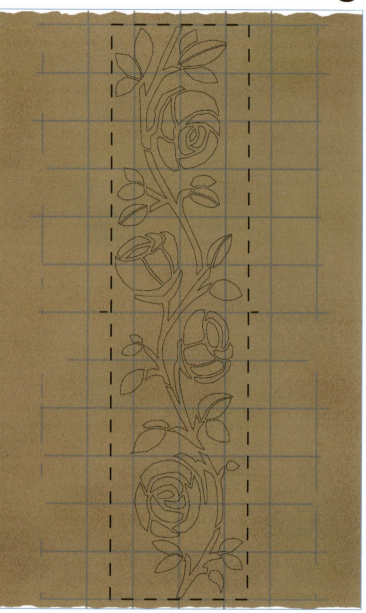

Scale, 2 units wide × 3 units high.

STEP 1
The Cartooned Stencil

Cartoon the complete wallpaper pattern on Kraft paper to create the master stencil.

- The complete wallpaper pattern is 9″ wide by 36″ long, and is represented by the dashed line on the example.

- The grid is 3″ squares.

- The pattern at the top of the stencil at the dashed line matches the pattern at the bottom of the stencil at the dashed line.

- Use a piece of Kraft paper (or any other paper the correct size) at least the size of the pattern.

- A medium-sized permanent marker will work well for cartooning this example.

- Alternatively, if the technology is available, scan the picture, size it in an image editor, and plot it out full size.

- Measure and draw the stencil pattern.

Titles in **bold** indicate paint names found on the elevation.

IMPORTANT!

- The scale on this page is 2 units wide × 3 units high; however, the image appears double the size of the other examples. This was done to make the stencil pattern easier to see and to duplicate.

NOTES

- There are two main sources for wallpaper and wallpaper pattern ideas: (1) commercial paint and decorating stores and (2) the Internet.

- Paint and decorating stores have a long history of selling wallpaper. Shelves of pattern books are usually divided by company and by type or function of the wallpaper.

- A scene shop might wish to stock a few of these books. Pattern books can usually be obtained when it is time for stores to replace obsolete books.

- These wallpaper patterns are also available on the Internet. These samples are typically at a low resolution but will provide design inspiration. Make sure the connection to cyberspace will allow the viewing of large amounts of data.

Things to Remember

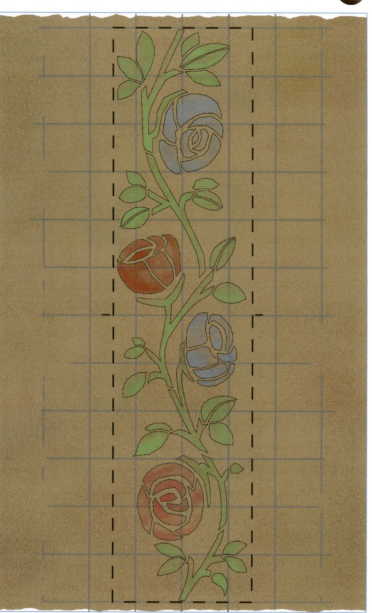

Scale, 2 units wide × 3 units high.

16

STEP 2
Colors for the Complete Stencil

Color the Kraft paper master stencil.

- Adding color is necessary for the creation of the individual stencils and stamps.

- Adding color will help to differentiate the various patterns on the master stencil.

- Colored pencil, marker, or even crayon will work well in applying the color.

- Work quickly. The color does not need to be precise as long the black lines are visible.

- This will serve as the master stencil once the color is applied. The stencil and stamps used for painting are executed using this design as a template.

Titles in **bold** indicate paint names found on the elevation.

IMPORTANT!

- The scale on this page is 2 units wide × 3 units high; however, the image appears double the size of other examples. This was done to make the stencil pattern easier to see and to duplicate.

> **NOTES**
>
> - Using real wallpaper might be practical if the designed wallpaper pattern is intricate or complicated.
>
> - A hard-covered flat is required for the application of wallpaper. Applying wallpaper on a traditional muslin flat is very difficult.
>
> - It might seem easier to apply wallpaper to horizontal flats in the shop; however, matching the wallpaper pattern in this situation can be challenging. It is probably safer to apply wallpaper when the set has been assembled.
>
> - Wallpaper can be expensive, and time, special equipment, and expertise are required when papering a set.

Things to Remember

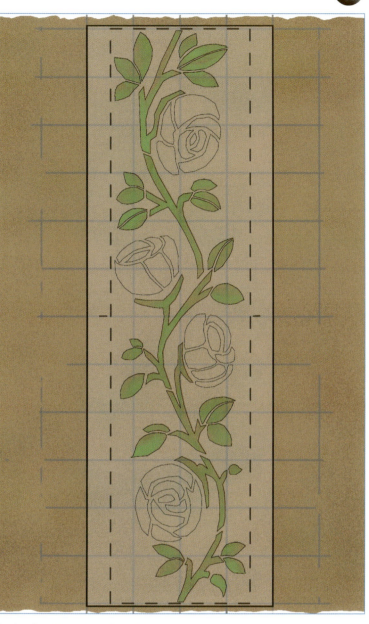

Scale, 2 units wide × 3 units high.

STEP 3
The Green Stencil

The material for the stencil can be a number of products. (See NOTES.)

- The stencil material in the example adds another 1-1/2″ on all sides. This will add strength to the stencil and allow room to paint without slopping over the edge of the material.
- The dashed lines represent a full stencil pattern that serves as a guide when painting.
- Material that is transparent or semitransparent will make it easier to transfer the stencil.

Place the material over the wallpaper pattern.

- Outline all the green areas with a marker.
- Draw the dashed line. These lines are used to line up the stencil.
- Cut out the marked areas using a matte knife or similar tool.

Titles in **bold** indicate paint names found on the elevation.

IMPORTANT!

- The scale on this page is 2 units wide × 3 units high; however, the image appears double the size of other examples. This was done to make the stencil pattern easier to see and to duplicate.

NOTES

- Materials for stencils could include:

  - Plastic (Mylar® or acetate will work well) is a thin material that is easy to cut but might not hold up through the entire project.

  - Stencil paper is easy to work with and it is easy to make multiple copies; however, stencil paper will break down quickly.

- Cover both sides of the Kraft paper pattern with clear packing tape or clear contact paper/shelf liner. Use a sharp knife to cut out the pieces.

- Bigger projects will require multiple stencils. Make sure to keep the master design for a wallpaper pattern.

Things to Remember

Scale, 2 units wide × 3 units high.

STEP 4
Stamps

Stamps can be used as an alternative to stencils. Make four stamps representing the four flowers in the project.

- Lay a piece of tracing paper or vellum over a flower.

- Use a marker to trace the flower on the paper.

- Cut out the individual shapes and lay them on a piece of foam rubber. Use a marker to outline the pieces on the foam. The foam rubber should be at least 1/2″ thick and could be even thicker.

- Cut out the pieces of foam rubber. Attach the pieces to a thin piece of plywood or Masonite®. Attach a dowel to the board as a handle. This handle can be inserted into a bamboo extension when painting on the floor.

- Lining up patterns can be tricky because the stamp is not transparent. Trim the board as close as possible to the applied foam. (See NOTES.)

- Transfer the pattern or mark the top of the stamp on the visible side. This mark is a way to line up the stamp when applying paint. [This might also help with clarity.]

Titles in **bold** indicate paint names found on the elevation.

IMPORTANT!

- The scale on this page is 2 units wide × 3 units high; however, the image appears double the size of other examples. This was done to make the stencil pattern easier to see and to duplicate.

NOTES

- A cafeteria tray or shallow baking tray is a good solution for loading paint on a stamp. Fill the tray with a small amount of paint and refill as needed.

- Take great care in laying out materials for painting. Locate all painting tools near the work area. Avoid placing materials in heavy traffic areas.

- A shallow pan with only a small amount of paint will help limit the damage should an accident happen.

- Test this application method before painting on scenery.

Things to Remember

Scale, 2 units wide × 3 units high.

STEP 5
Base Paint and Spatter

Base paint the flat with the **Base**.

- If this flat has been used, the paint should be just thick enough to cover the previous painting project.

- If this is a new flat, the paint should be just thick enough to cover the flat.

- In either case, remember that a lot of additional paint will go on this flat. Only a small amount of paint is needed.

- Dip the brush in a small amount of paint. Remember to use the tips of the brush.

- Use an omnidirectional brush stroke when base painting.

- Avoid holidays.

Use a 3″ or 4″ brush to paint the spatter. This is a good time to use an old brush that might not be good for anything else.

- Start painting with **Spatter #1**.

- Dip the brush in the paint and use the side of the bucket to remove excess paint from the brush, then swipe the brush on the floor or other approved area to remove even more excess.

- Repeat the process with **Spatter #2** and **Spatter #3**.

Titles in **bold** indicate paint names found on the **elevation**.

NOTES

- The consistency of the spatter paint should be DILUTED. If the paint is too thick, it will stay on the brush. If the paint is too thin, it will not read very well on the finished flat.

- There are many ways of applying spatter. One method is to hit the spatter brush against a stick or hand to control the application. Flicking the wrist in the direction of the painting surface but avoiding back-snap is another possibility. Wildly swinging the brush is likely to deposit paint on all adjacent surfaces, including coworkers. This will make the supervisors upset.

- This is a small area to spatter. A sprayer can be used for larger projects.

16

STEP 6
Cartoon and Spatter the Stripes

Paint the striped wallpaper on the flat. (See NOTES.)

- Measure and cartoon the vertical lines. The wallpaper stripes are 9″ wide and the space between the stripes is 6″ wide.

- Cover (or mask) the 6″ stripes so the spatter will only hit the 9″-wide areas.

- The stripes are created by covering the area with paper, tape, or lumber. Determine what material is available and will work the best to create the stripes.

Paint the stripes.

- With the 6″ stripes covered, spatter the flat with **Spatter #4**. This will create a different background for the wallpaper stripes.

Titles in **bold** indicate paint names found on the elevation.

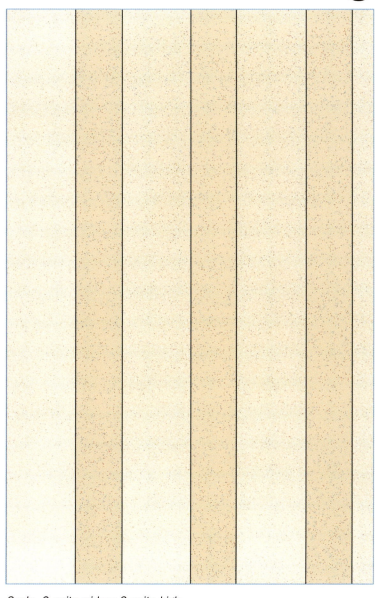

Scale, 2 units wide × 3 units high.

IMPORTANT!
- The cartoon lines in the example are black for clarity. Consider using chalk instead of charcoal. The cartoon lines might not be needed if 6″ wide pieces of Kraft paper or plywood are used for masking.

NOTES

- This project is painted in a *trompe l'oeil* painting style.

- *Trompe l'oeil* is French for "to fool (or deceive) the eye."

- *Trompe l'oeil* techniques were developed in Italy during the Rococo period.

- Painting with perspective and foreshortening plus highlight and shadow are typical of the *trompe l'oeil* style.

- The goal is for audience members to believe that they are seeing objects in three dimensions when they are viewing a two-dimensional surface.

Things to Remember

16

STEP 7
Paint the Green Layer

Line up the stencil.

- Start at the top and right of the flat.

- Place the stencil on the flat. The dashed lines on the stencil line up with the vertical paint lines on the flat. The top edge of the stencil lines up with the edge of the flat.

Paint the flat through the stencil with **Wallpaper green**.

- Use a stipple brush, sponge, or a disposable foam brush. (See NOTES.)

- Dip the applicator of choice into a small amount of paint. Dab the applicator a number of times on a test surface to evenly distribute the paint and to remove most of the paint on the applicator.

- Paint through the stencil and onto the flat. Try to work from the edges of the stencil toward the center of each small, cutout area. This will help prevent the accumulation of paint at the edges of the stencil.

Move the stencil and paint to the next pattern. This pattern starts in the middle of the stencil.

- Place the two marks in the middle of the stencil at the top of the flat to start the second pattern. The next application will connect as usual.

Titles in **bold** indicate paint names found on the elevation.

Scale, 2 units wide × 3 units high.

16

> **NOTES**
>
> - A stippling brush (a round brush with short bristles cut flat on the end) can be used for applying paint. This brush is used for dabbing paint rather than brushing paint. This brush has limited uses and can be difficult to master.
>
> - A natural sponge, a synthetic sponge, a foam brush, or even pieces of foam rubber are all possibilities for paint application.
>
> - Paint will build up on the edges of the negative spaces. The stencils should be cleaned on a regular basis, possibly after every application.
>
> - The trick to painting with a stencil is to use as little paint as possible. Paint will tend to wick under the edges of the stencil when large quantities of paint are used.

Things to Remember

STEP 8
Paint the Stamps

Use **Wallpaper blue**, **Wallpaper red**, and **Wallpaper rust** to paint the stamps. Lining up stamp patterns can be tricky. Stamps are best used for applications that do not require precise alignment. Foliage is an example. In this case, the stamp must fit with the stencil.

- The stencil pattern is designed with unpainted areas for easy stamp alignment.

- Duplicate the stamp pattern on the side of the stamp that is visible.

- Mark the visible side of the stamp with guide marks that will aid in consistent application.

- Trim the board as close as possible to the applied foam.

Load the stamp with paint.

- The paint should be the DILUTED consistency.

- Do not overload the stamp. Excess paint will result in a blotchy application.

- One paint load should last for multiple stamp applications.

- Jump around the flat at random when stamping each individual color; otherwise, a distinct pattern will develop as the paint runs out. (See NOTES.)

Titles in **bold** indicate paint names found on the elevation.

Scale, 2 units wide × 3 units high.

16

> **NOTES**
>
> - A cafeteria tray or shallow baking tray is a good solution for loading paint on a stamp. Fill the tray with a small amount of paint and refill as needed.
>
> - Take great care in laying out materials for painting.
>
> - Press the stamp on another surface before applying paint to the finished surface. This will eliminate excess paint and avoid a blotchy stamp application.
>
> - Not all of the stamp applications have to match exactly. Press with lighter pressure at the beginning of a load and slightly increase the pressure as the paint is used.
>
> - Pressing too hard will allow the board to contact the surface and distort the pattern. Load additional paint on the stamp before this happens.

Things to Remember

STEP 9
Enhance the Wallpaper Stencil and Stamps

The painted wallpaper pattern looks a bit uninteresting. An application of **Shadow wash** will help. This is accomplished in one of two ways.

Use a brush:

- Use a small brush and **Shadow wash** to paint the detail. The wash is applied to the left and the underneath of the stencil and stamps.

- This method will be less regular. It will be difficult to exactly duplicate the same brush strokes from one pattern to another.

- This technique might be difficult to use on a large project.

Use the stencil:

- Cut out the flower area from the green stencil pattern.

- Use this new stencil and **Shadow wash** to paint this detail.

- Place the stencil slightly to the left and beneath the painted wallpaper pattern.

- Mask the area around the stencil with Kraft paper.

- Spatter or spray a small amount of paint through the stencil.

Titles in **bold** indicate paint names found on the elevation.

Scale, 2 units wide × 3 units high.

NOTES

- The addition of a dark wash for this step is not done to imply a realistic shadow. The wallpaper pattern does not have dimension and therefore will not cast a shadow.

- This application simply adds interest to the wallpaper to make it more interesting.

- Check out actual wallpaper at paint and decoration stores for evidence of the same technique.

- Practice mixing and using washes. This technique *must* be mastered. Washes are used in almost every project. It will take practice.

- Please test all paints, especially washes. Darker washes will tend to dry with less intensity and lighter washes will tend to dry with more intensity (but it is very unpredictable).

- Stir this paint often. It will settle more than paint of regular consistency.

Things to Remember

16

STEP 10
Paint the Areas Between the Stenciled Wallpaper Stripes, Including Highlight and Shadow

Add small stripes to the areas between the **stenciled** wallpaper stripes with **Spatter #4** and a straightedge. (See NOTES.)

- Place the straightedge 1/4″ from the **stenciled** wallpaper stripe. Use a 3/4″ brush to dry brush this line. Now place the straightedge 1/4″ from the new painted line. Use a 1/4″ brush to paint this line. (See the detail in the example.)

- Repeat this process on the other side of the **stenciled** wallpaper stripe.

Paint the texture pattern in the **areas between the stenciled wallpaper stripes**.

- This can be accomplished with a 2-1/2″ brush or a textured roller.

Finishing touches:

- Paint a sharp cutline of **Highlight wash** on the right side of each **stenciled** wallpaper stripe. (See NOTES.)

- Paint a sharp cutline of **Shadow wash** on the left side of each **stenciled** wallpaper stripe.

Titles in **bold** indicate paint names found on the elevation.

Scale, 2 units wide × 3 units high.

NOTES
- The goal of a scenic artist is to duplicate the paint elevation. The pattern between the **stenciled** wallpaper stripes is very subtle. (See the detail in the example.) This allows the painter a degree of freedom in determining the best approach for application.

- Measuring for brush size is a suggestion.

- Painting a test flat is the best way to explore the choices of tools and techniques required to complete this project.

- The **stenciled** wallpaper stripe will not cast a shadow. The lines of wash will help separate the **stenciled** wallpaper pattern from the other stripes. These cutlines are very subtle. Please test this application.

16

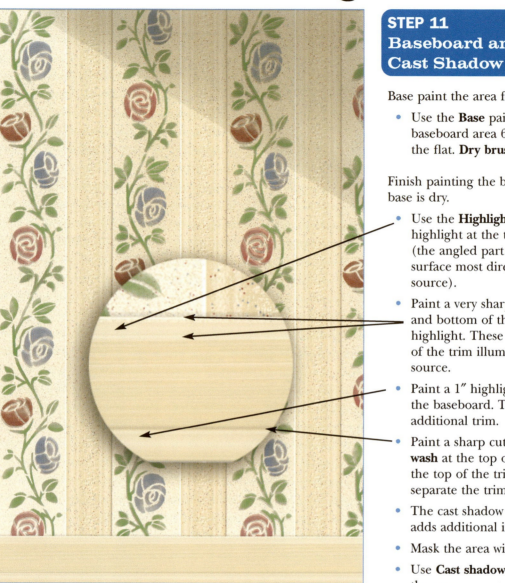

Scale, 2 units wide × 3 units high.

STEP 11
Baseboard and
Cast Shadow

Base paint the area for the baseboard.

- Use the **Base** paint color to paint the baseboard area 6″ from the bottom of the flat. **Dry brush with Spatter #4.**

Finish painting the baseboard when the base is dry.

- Use the **Highlight wash** to paint a 3/4″ highlight at the top of the baseboard (the angled part of the trim and the surface most direct to the light source).

- Paint a very sharp cutline on the top and bottom of the baseboard highlight. These are the sharp edges of the trim illuminated by the light source.

- Paint a 1″ highlight at the bottom of the baseboard. This represents additional trim.

- Paint a sharp cutline with the **Shadow wash** at the top of the baseboard and the top of the trim. This will help to separate the trim from the wall.

- The cast shadow at the top of the flat adds additional interest to the project.

- Mask the area with Kraft paper.

- Use **Cast shadow** to spatter or spray the area.

Titles in **bold** indicate paint names found on the elevation.

IMPORTANT!

- This line is very subtle and barely noticeable. Be very careful not to paint it too big or too dark. (See NOTES.)

NOTES

- The bright edge reflection should be the same color as the **Highlight wash**. Rather than mix a new color or consistency, use a bit of the **Highlight wash** that has settled in the bottom of the container.

- The same is true for the sharp shadow cutline.

- **P.S.** Items could hang on the wall. Light fixtures, a shelf with decorative items, or even a painting could be a challenging next step.

- Drapery could be painted over this wallpapered wall (see Project 17).

Things to Remember

WORK SURFACE

A 4′ × 6′ traditional or hard-covered flat.

TYPE OF PAINT

Rosco *Off Broadway* paint, Rosco *Iddings Deep Colors*, or a commercial latex substitute. See the COLOR SAMPLES page at the beginning of this book for brand and color suggestions.

TYPES OF CONSISTENCY

OUT OF THE CAN—Rosco suggests that the paint can be used right out of the can. This consistency might be thick. Add water to achieve a NORMAL consistency (see below).

NORMAL—Thick enough just to cover other projects in a single coat, assuming that the difference between the paint colors is not too great.

DILUTED—1 or 2 parts paint to 1 part water added to the NORMAL paint consistency.

WATERY—1 part paint to 5 to 10 parts water added to the NORMAL paint consistency. Rosco says: "Diluting with more than 2 parts water may reduce binder strength. Add Rosco *Clear Acrylic Glaze* to restore adhesion and flexibility."

PAINTING TECHNIQUES

GRADED WET BLEND (paint technique)—Arranged in a scale or series; a smooth blend of gradated colors, usually in a linear pattern.

CARTOON—A line drawing of a paint elevation used as a guide for a painting project.

WET BLEND (paint technique)—Combining two or more colors on a painting surface while still wet.

SHADOW WASH (paint technique)—A dark, transparent paint used to suggest a shadow cast from one object on another.

HIGHLIGHT WASH (paint technique)—A light, translucent paint used to represent the reflection of light or an area that receives the greatest amount of illumination.

Glossary

BLEND—To combine so that the line of demarcation cannot be distinguished.

VALANCE—A short drapery or piece of wood used as a decorative heading to conceal the tops of curtains and fixtures.

CORD (decorative)—A long slender flexible material usually consisting of several strands of thread or yarn woven or twisted together.

BRUSH COMB—Tool used for cleaning brushes.

CHALK—A stick of soft white or buff limestone composed chiefly of the shells of foraminifers.

CHARCOAL (VINE)—A stick of fine charred softwood used in drawing.

GRADIENT—The rate of graded ascent or descent.

PAINT ELEVATION—A scaled, color drawing or painting of a piece of scenery provided by the scenic designer.

SCENIC FITCH—A scenic brush with a long, wooden handle and an oval-shaped ferrule.

STRAIGHTEDGE—A straight length of wood with a handle that ensures the painting of a straight line.

Scale, 2 units wide × 3 units high.

TOOLS NEEDED
(See the Project pages for details.)

- **A collection of scene and housepainting brushes**
- **Chalk or charcoal for cartooning**
- **Tape measure**
- **Straightedge or lining stick**

Gradient #1 Cool gray - medium	**Drape dark** Ultramarine blue - dark	**Trim #2** Lemon yellow
Gradient #2 Cool gray - medium light	**Trim base** Burnt sienna	**Highlight wash** White/blue - 10% opacity
Gradient #3 Cool gray - light	**Trim light** Raw sienna	**Shadow wash** Black - 10% opacity
Drape base Ultramarine blue	**Trim dark** Burnt umber	
Drape light Ultramarine blue - medium	**Trim #1** Yellow ochre	

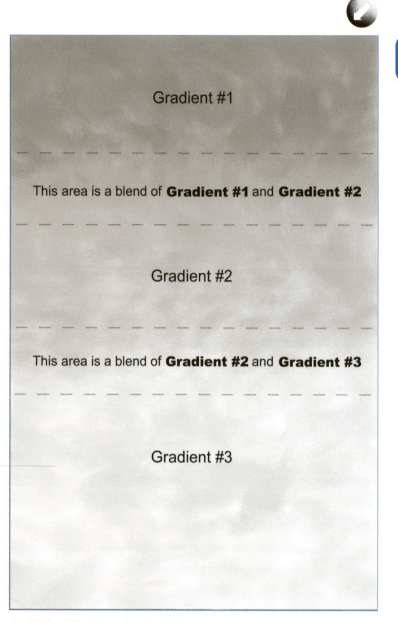

Gradient #1

This area is a blend of **Gradient #1** and **Gradient #2**

Gradient #2

This area is a blend of **Gradient #2** and **Gradient #3**

Gradient #3

Scale, 2 units wide × 3 units high.

STEP 1
Gradient Background

Prepare the paint used for the graded wet blend: **Gradient #1**, **Gradient #2**, and **Gradient #3**.

- These paints should be NORMAL consistency. (See NOTES.)

The purpose of the graded wet blend is to achieve an even progression from one color to another.

- Divide the flat into three horizontal sections.
- The bottom section is the largest.
- Base the top section with **Gradient #1**, including the top half of the area labeled "This area is a blend of **Gradient #1** and **Gradient #2**."
- Base the middle section with **Gradient #2**, including the bottom half of that blended area. These paints should almost touch.

Now blend these two colors before the paint has a chance to dry. (See NOTES.)

- Use a clean, damp brush for the blending.
- Work quickly and use a light stroke.
- Don't overwork this technique.

Repeat this procedure with the next two areas and use **Gradient #2** and **Gradient #3**. (See NOTES.)

Titles in **bold** indicate paint names found on the elevation.

NOTES

- Mixing equal parts of **Gradient #1** and **Gradient #3** will produce **Gradient #2**. When the paint is correctly mixed, place a drop of one color in the other buckets. A drop of the other colors will not affect the original color of the paint.

- If **Gradient #2** is dry when beginning to blend **Gradients #2** and **#3**, re-base the bottom of the second section with **Gradient #2**.

- If brush strokes are noticeable and too rough after the blend, smooth out this area. While the paint is still wet, use a clean, damp 4″ brush to gently blend the paint on a horizontal line.

STEP 2
Cartoon the Drapery

Cartoon the area that will be the drapery.

- Use chalk or charcoal to cartoon the flat.

- Please measure very carefully. Many projects are ruined because of mistakes made in measurement.

- There are many ways to approach cartooning a flat. Using a grid for this project might be a good idea. (See NOTES.)

- Check Steps 2 and 3 in Project 6 for additional details.

Make every attempt to exactly copy the example.

- There is some leeway in the cartooning process because of the fluid nature of fabric.

- The wet blend process will also add to the flexible nature of the cartoon process.

Titles in **bold** indicate paint names found on the elevation.

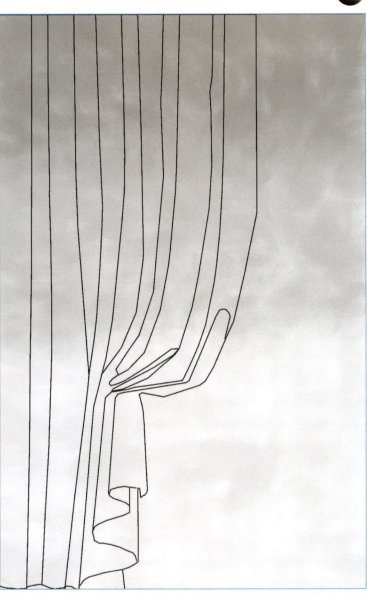

Scale, 2 units wide × 3 units high.

NOTES

- A grid is a useful method for cartooning when the shapes drawn are natural and nonarchitectural.

- A grid with 1′ squares is small but will work well for this project. A bigger grid should be constructed on larger projects, such as a full drop.

- The blue or red chalk found in most shop snap lines will be difficult to remove from the flat. A new snap line filled with charcoal power is a great addition to scene painting equipment.

- Consider labeling the grid lines when working with a large project.

Scale, 2 units wide × 3 units high.

STEP 3
Base and Wet Blend the Drapery

For this step, use **Drape base**, **Drape dark**, and **Drape light**.

Base one of the inner drapery pleats.

- Use a smaller brush to base the area.

- While the base paint is still wet, paint the right side of the pleat with **Drape dark** and the left side of the pleat with **Drape light**. (See NOTES.)

- Have a fairly clean brush handy in case it is needed to blend the drape surface. The base brush might also work for this purpose.

Base one of the outer drapery pleats.

- Use a 4″ brush to base the area.

- While the base paint is still wet, paint the left side of the pleat with **Drape dark** and the right side of the pleat with **Drape light**.

- Have a fairly clean brush handy in case it is needed to blend the drape surface.

- Use less **Drape light** on the inner pleats and less **Drape dark** on the outer pleats.

Don't work too hard to get a perfect blend from the three paints. The effect will be lost if the paint is excessively blended.

- Continue the process and finish painting the entire drape. Use an appropriate-size brush for all the areas.

Titles in **bold** indicate paint names found on the elevation.

NOTES

- Because the right side of the inner pleat is the most hidden from the light, it is painted with the darker paint.

- Because the right side of the outer pleat receives the most light, it is painted with the lighter paint.

- It is important to paint these areas while the paint is still wet, so this is a reasonably quick technique.

Things to Remember

Scale, 2 units wide × 3 units high.

STEP 4
Cartoon and Base the Valance

Use chalk or charcoal to cartoon the flat.

- Please measure very carefully. Many projects are ruined because of mistakes made in measurement.
- Cartoon the outline of the valance, then base paint that area.
- Cartoon the remainder of the valance area after the base is completely dry.

Titles in **bold** indicate paint names found on the elevation.

IMPORTANT!
- The main drape is lightened in this example. The valance is easier to see as a result.

NOTES

- When cartooning a flat, use chalk or other light-color material on dark surfaces.

- When cartooning a flat, use vine charcoal or other dark material on light surfaces.

- Make sure that whatever is used can be removed or covered up when the cartoon lines are no longer needed.

- Remember, some materials (such as marker) will not always cover with paint. This might be a problem with the current project and might be a real problem when moving to the next project.

Things to Remember

Scale, 2 units wide × 3 units high.

STEP 5
Wet Blend the Valance

For this step use **Drape base**, **Drape dark**, and **Drape light**.

- While the base paint is still wet, paint the right side of the inner pleat with **Drape dark** and the left side of the inner pleat with **Drape light**.

- Have a fairly clean brush handy in case it is needed to blend the drape surface. The base brush might also work for this purpose.

- While the base paint is still wet, paint the left side of the outer pleat with **Drape dark** and the right side of the outer pleat with **Drape light**.

- Have a fairly clean brush handy in case it is needed to blend the drape surface.

- Use less **Drape light** on the inner pleats and less **Drape dark** on the outer pleats.

Don't work too hard to get a perfect blend from the three paints. The effect will be lost if the paint is excessively blended.

- Continue the process and finish painting the entire drape. Use an appropriate-size brush for all the areas.

Titles in **bold** indicate paint names found on the elevation.

IMPORTANT!
- The main drape is lightened in this example. The valance is easier to see as a result.

NOTES

- Mood and attitude affect the quality of scene painting. Plan ahead and try to avoid a last-minute rush.

- How long should it take to paint a project? Each painter is different, so there is no one correct answer. Remember that most scenery is viewed from a distance. Don't spend time laboring over minute detail that an audience will not see.

- Many painters find that working with others is more enjoyable then painting alone.

- Music is often a good choice as long as it doesn't interfere with work or with communication. Consider rotating the choice of music selections among all of the workers.

Things to Remember

Scale, 2 units wide × 3 units high.

STEP 6
Fringe Base

Prepare the **Trim base**, **Trim light**, and **Trim dark**. Use these colors for the base of the fringe.

- The paint should be the NORMAL consistency with a bit more water. This will aid in the blending process.

Use an appropriate-size brush to paint each fringe section with the **Trim base**.

- Apply the two trim colors, **Trim light** and **Trim dark**, while the base paint is still wet.

- Work one fringe section at a time and work quickly.

- Either use three brushes or clean the brush out a bit after applying each color.

Please look at the example.

- Remember the direction of the light. This base will begin to give the fringe areas dimension.

- The side of the fringe base most hidden from the light is painted with the darker paint.

- The side of the fringe base receiving the most light is painted with the lighter paint.

- The cartoon lines around each fringe section are visible in this example to make each area easier to see. They should be covered with paint when completing this step.

Titles in **bold** indicate paint names found on the elevation.

NOTES

- Scene painting brushes are expensive, aren't they? Always leave enough time at the end of a painting session for proper cleanup, especially brush cleanup.

- Don't soak paint brushes. Soaking can cause bristles to droop, ferrules to rust, and handles to swell.

- Use lukewarm water and a mild soap to clean brushes.

- A wire brush can harm the bristles and even pull them out from the ferrule. Use a brush comb specifically intended for fine brushes.

- Place the brush back in its plastic keeper. If the brush did not come in one, use a piece of paper towel to gently wrap the bristles.

Things to Remember

STEP 7
Fringe Detail

Now paint the fringe. When painting fringe, start with the darker colors. Add a bit more water to the NORMAL consistency. Start with **Trim black** (not on the elevation, but it is a straight black paint). Continue painting with the remainder of the colors. As the paint gets lighter, paint fewer lines in each color.

Add **Trim Black**.

Add **Trim dark**.

Add **Trim base**.

Add **Trim light**.

Add **Trim #1**.

Add **Trim #2**.

STEP 8
Cord and Tassels

Cartoon the area that will become the cords and tassels.

Prepare the **Trim base**, **Trim light**, and **Trim dark**. Use these colors for the base of the cord and tassels.

- The paint should be the NORMAL consistency with a bit more water. This will aid in the blending process.

Paint the cords.

- Use the **Trim base** to base paint the cords.

- Paint the sides of the cords that are toward the light with a small line of **Trim light**.

- Paint the sides of the cords that are away from the light with a small line of **Trim dark**. (See lower insert on the example.)

- Use **Trim #1** yellow ochre to paint the cords with an "S"-shaped brush stroke. (See NOTES.)

- Paint the edge of the cord toward the light with **Trim #2**. Start the "S" brush stroke but stop before getting to the middle of the cord.

- Paint the edge of the cord away from the light with **Trim dark**. Start the "S" brush stroke in the middle of the cord. (See upper insert on the example.)

- Paint the tassels using the same procedure found on the previous page.

Titles in **bold** indicate paint names found on the elevation.

Scale, 2 units wide × 3 units high.

NOTES

- When painting cord, use an "S"-shaped brush stroke.
- Start the brush stroke in the direction of the cord.
- Continue the stroke on a slight angle.
- Finish the stroke in the direction of the cord.
- Always keep the edge of the brush running in the same direction as the cord, even on a curve.

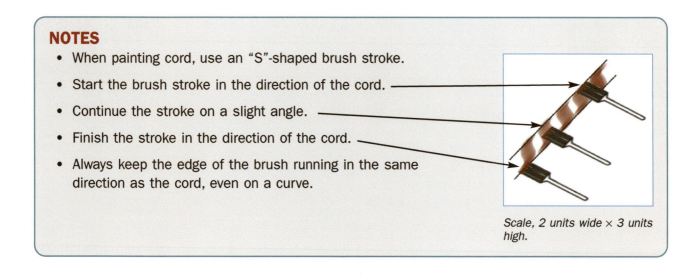

Scale, 2 units wide × 3 units high.

Things to Remember

STEP 9
Shadow

Look at the example to the right.
Use the **Shadow wash** to paint the shadows:

- A deep cast shadow between the pleats
- A blended shadow on either side
- A cast shadow (which curves because the drapery is curved; it will not distort on the wall)
- A cast shadow on the drapery (by the cord)
- A cast shadow between the pleats
- A cast shadow on the wall (by the cord and tassel)
- A cast shadow on the cord (by the cord)
- A cast shadow on the drapery (by the cord)
- A cast shadow on the drapery (by the cord)
- A deep cast shadow between the pleats
- A cast shadow (by the fringe)
- A cast shadow (by the tassels)

Titles in **bold** indicate paint names found on the elevation.

Scale, 2 units wide × 3 units high.

IMPORTANT!
- The **Shadow wash** is critical for the success of this project. Please test the paint.

NOTES
- Practice mixing and using washes. This technique *must* be mastered. Washes are used in almost every project. It will take practice.
- Please test all paints, especially washes. Darker washes will tend to dry with less intensity and lighter washes will tend to dry with more intensity (but it is very unpredictable).
- A small flat (maybe 2′ × 3′) will work well as a test flat.
- Stir this paint often. It will settle more than paint of NORMAL consistency.

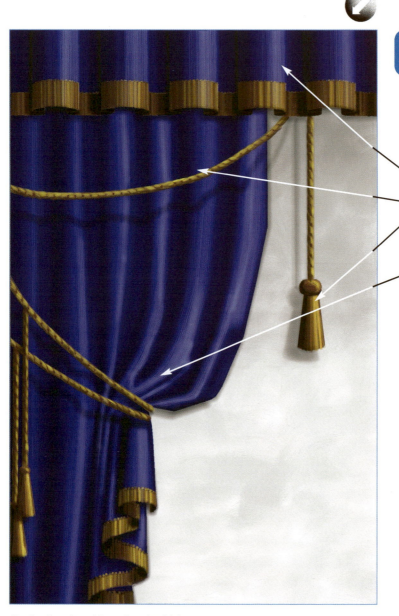

Scale, 2 units wide × 3 units high.

STEP 10
Highlight

Look at the example to the right.
  Use the **Highlight wash** to paint the highlights:

- A small highlight on the pleats of the valance (note that they are not consistent for every pleat)

- A few highlights in the cord

- A small bit in the tassels

- A small highlight on the pleats of the drapery (note that they are not consistent for every pleat)

Titles in **bold** indicate paint names found on the elevation.

IMPORTANT!

- All the highlights in this project are subtle.

- At this stage of the project, a bright, untested highlight will spoil all the work. It would be better to omit the highlight rather than have it be too bright.

- Have a bucket of clean water for blending if necessary.

NOTES

- **P.S.** There is not a lot to add to this project. It is possible that all the cords, tassels, and fringes could be more ornate.

- This drapery project could be painted on many of the projects in this book.

- Drapery painted over the bookshelf or the marble would look excellent, and the result would be a very complicated project.

Things to Remember

PROJECT 18

Flat Construction and Preparation

WORK SURFACE

A $4' \times 6'$ traditional or hard-covered flat.

Glossary

RAIL—An element of standard flat construction; the top and bottom pieces of wood used to build a flat frame.

STILE—An element of standard flat construction; the side pieces of wood used to build a flat frame.

TOGGLE—An element of standard flat construction; pieces of wood used for internal structural stability.

CORNER BRACE—An element of standard flat construction; the diagonal members used to keep the flat frame square.

CORNER BLOCK—An element of standard flat construction; a right-triangle piece of plywood used to secure the 90° joint of the rail and stile of a flat frame.

KEYSTONE—An element of standard flat construction; a piece of plywood (slightly wider on one end) used to secure a toggle to a rail or stile.

STRAP—An element of standard flat construction; a rectangular piece of plywood used to secure a toggle to a rail or stile.

HALF-STRAP—An element of standard flat construction; a trapezoid-shaped piece of plywood used to fasten a diagonal brace to the rail or stile.

MUSLIN—Fabric used to cover flats.

CHAMFER—A 45° bevel on the edge of plywood fasteners.

LAUNDRY STARCH—A traditional and inexpensive primer used for priming flats.

WALL SIZE—A commercial product found in paint and hardware stores; used for priming flats.

ANIMAL GLUE—Long used as a binder for dry pigment paints; also used as a primer.

WHITE GLUE—Popular commercial glue.

BRUSH—Device composed of bristles typically set into a handle and used especially for sweeping, smoothing, scrubbing, or painting.

FLAT—A wooden frame secured with plywood fasteners and covered with material; a lighter alternative to a solid wall.

HARD COVERED FLAT—A wooden frame secured with plywood fasteners and covered with a solid material (lauan, plywood, or Masonite®); an alternative to a traditional flat.

BEVEL—A sloping part or surface.

LAUAN—Any of various types of tropical plywood. The name "lauan" comes from trees found in the Philippines but it has become a generic term in the United States for imported tropical plywood.

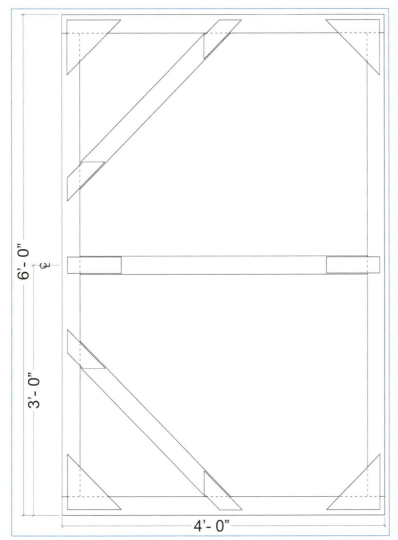

Scale, 1″ = 1′, or 2 units wide × 3 units high.

6'- 0"

3'- 0"

4'- 0"

TOOLS NEEDED
(See the Project pages for details.)

- Assorted saws
- Hammer
- Tool for inserting screws
- Nails or screws
- Scraps of wood
- Glue and size
- Utility knife
- Buckets
- Old paint brushes

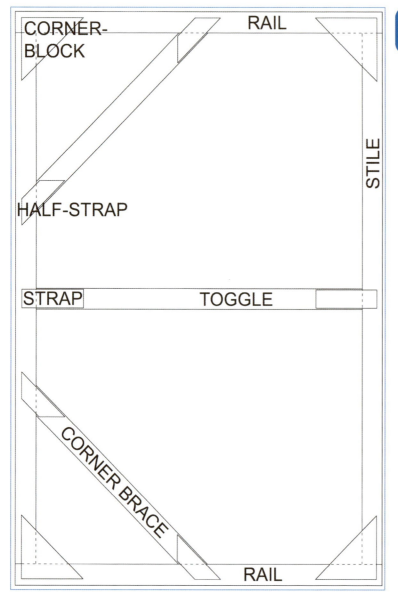

Scale, 1″ = 1′, or 2 units wide × 3 units high.

A traditional flat frame has four parts:

- Rails—The horizontal top and bottom members of a flat; two are needed.

- Stiles—The vertical side members of a flat; two are needed.

- Toggle—The horizontal members inside the flat frame; one is needed. (See NOTES.)

- Corner braces—The diagonal members used to keep the flat frame square; two are needed. (See NOTES.)

These pieces are joined with plywood fasteners:

- Corner block—Connects the corners of the flat frame.

- Strap—Connects the toggle to the stile.

- Half-strap—Connects the corner brace to the rail and stile.

- Keystone—Connects the toggle to the stile. (See NOTES.)

Chamfer the edges of all the plywood fasteners. A 45° bevel on the edges:

- Helps to lessen splinters and slivers.

- Reduces the chances of snagging costumes.

- Makes flat handling and storage easier because the flats will slide next to each other with less chance of tearing. (See NOTES.)

NOTES

- The number of toggles will vary depending on the finished height of the flat frame. Vertical distances greater than 4′ require a toggle. Additional toggles are added to accommodate the addition of scenic elements, such as moldings, openings, and trim.

- Corner braces are used for flat frames 4′ and wider. They are always attached on the same side to the same stile. It does not matter which stile; either is acceptable.

- The trapezoid shape of a keystone adds additional width on the end that fastens to the stile. The result is a stronger flat frame. This shape takes longer to make and uses more material. This fastener is seldom used in contemporary flat construction.

- If lack of time is a factor in flat building, chamfering is usually eliminated.

Things to Remember

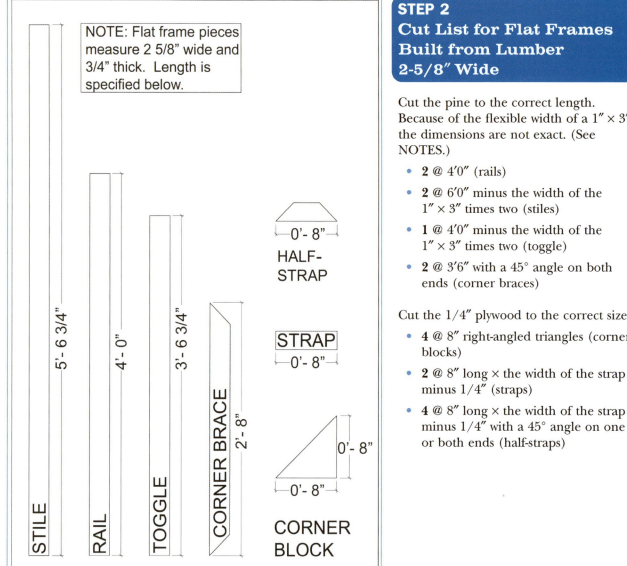

NOTE: Flat frame pieces measure 2 5/8" wide and 3/4" thick. Length is specified below.

STILE — 5'- 6 3/4"

RAIL — 4'- 0"

TOGGLE — 3'- 6 3/4"

CORNER BRACE — 2'- 8"

HALF-STRAP — 0'- 8"

STRAP — 0'- 8"

CORNER BLOCK — 0'- 8" × 0'- 8"

Scale, 1" = 1', or 2 units wide × 3 units high.

STEP 2
Cut List for Flat Frames Built from Lumber 2-5/8" Wide

Cut the pine to the correct length. Because of the flexible width of a 1" × 3", the dimensions are not exact. (See NOTES.)

- **2 @ 4'0"** (rails)
- **2 @ 6'0"** minus the width of the 1" × 3" times two (stiles)
- **1 @ 4'0"** minus the width of the 1" × 3" times two (toggle)
- **2 @ 3'6"** with a 45° angle on both ends (corner braces)

Cut the 1/4" plywood to the correct size:

- **4 @ 8"** right-angled triangles (corner blocks)
- **2 @ 8"** long × the width of the strap minus 1/4" (straps)
- **4 @ 8"** long × the width of the strap minus 1/4" with a 45° angle on one or both ends (half-straps)

IMPORTANT!
- The edges of toggles and corner braces can cause a problem when painting a traditional flat. Excess painting pressure will create a paint line at those edges. There are many techniques to eliminate this problem. Inserting a 1/8" shim between the flat frame and the straps during construction will create a gap between the toggle and corner braces. The sure-fire solution is to use a hard-covered flat instead.

18

NOTES

- What is a 1″ × 3″ really? This is a good and reasonable question. Lumber has a *nominal size* and an *actual size*. The nominal size (think "name") is the common reference—in this case, a "1 × 3." The actual thickness of a 1 × 3 is only 3/4″ . . . but how wide is it? There are four possible answers:

  - The width could really be a true 3″.

  - The width could be 2-3/4″, a dimension typical when receiving 1 × 3's from a lumber supply company.

  - The width could be 2-5/8″. This dimension provides for the least amount of waste when ripping a 1″ × 12″ into multiple 1″ × 3″ pieces.

  - The width could be 2-1/2″. This dimension seems to be the easiest to calculate and measure but provides the least amount of strength.

Things to Remember

18

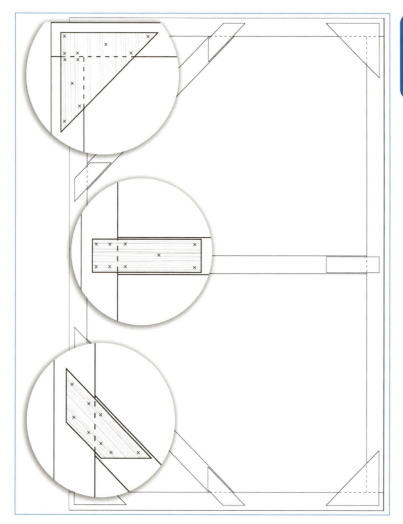

Scale, 1" = 1', or 2 units wide × 3 units high.

STEP 3
Nailing Patterns and the Direction of the Plywood Grain

Cut 1/4″ plywood to construct fasteners. Corner blocks are made in two different ways:

- Using a radial arm saw, cut a 45° angle on a strip of plywood 8″ wide. Flip the strip over. Cut again at the first cut. Repeat. This produces a corner block with grain running parallel with the hypotenuse.

- Cut perfect squares from a strip of plywood 8″ wide, then cut across the diagonal. This produces a corner block with the grain running parallel with the short side. The grain must run perpendicular to the seam of the joint when using this corner block.

Straps replace keystones most of the time:

- The width of the plywood strap is 1/4″ less than the width of the 1 × 3.

- The strap is usually 8″ long.

- Half-straps are used to attach the corner braces. They have a 45° angle on one or both ends as a result.

- Indent all plywood fasteners 3/4″ from the outside edge of the flat frame. (See NOTES.)

NOTES

- Always indent the plywood fasteners 3/4″ from the edge of the flat frame (or the thickness of the lumber used for the frame).

- This indent will allow one flat to attach flush to another flat when creating an outside corner.

- Few stagecraft problems are as annoying as ill-fitting flats because of an incorrect indent.

STEP 4
Assembling the Flat Frame

A flat rides on its rails.

- Rails extend the full width of the flat. There would be a risk of splitting wood if the stiles went all the way to the floor.

A large work table with access around the entire table is a great way to build a flat. The floor will also work.

- Use nails to attach the frame to the table or floor if permitted. Partially sunk common nails or duplex nails work well. Pull the nails out after construction. It is also possible to construct the frame without attaching it to a surface.

- Use a framing square to line up the corners. (See NOTES.)

- Draw a 3/4″ line from the edge of the flat at all the places a fastener is attached. A scrap of 1 × 3 on edge works well as a guide.

- Apply glue on the back of a corner block and place on the corner of the flat. Don't go over the lines. (See NOTES.)

- Use the pattern in the example to attach the corner block. Use nails, screws, or staples. Make sure they are smaller than 1″. An ideal length is 7/8″.

- Repeat the process for the other corner blocks.

- Use the pattern in the example to attach the toggle and the corner braces.

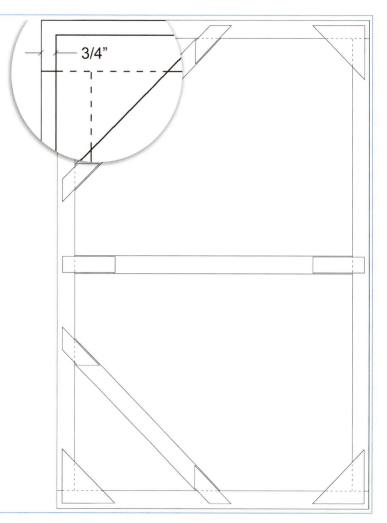

Scale, 1″ = 1′, or 2 units wide × 3 units high.

NOTES

- Measure the flat frame on the diagonal from opposite corners. Now measure the other diagonal. If the frame is square, the two dimensions will be equal.

- Glue the plywood fasteners if the finished flat is used as stock and will go into storage for another production.

- Don't use glue to attach plywood fasteners if the flat is to be disassembled. Use screws to attach the fasteners. They are easier to strike.

18

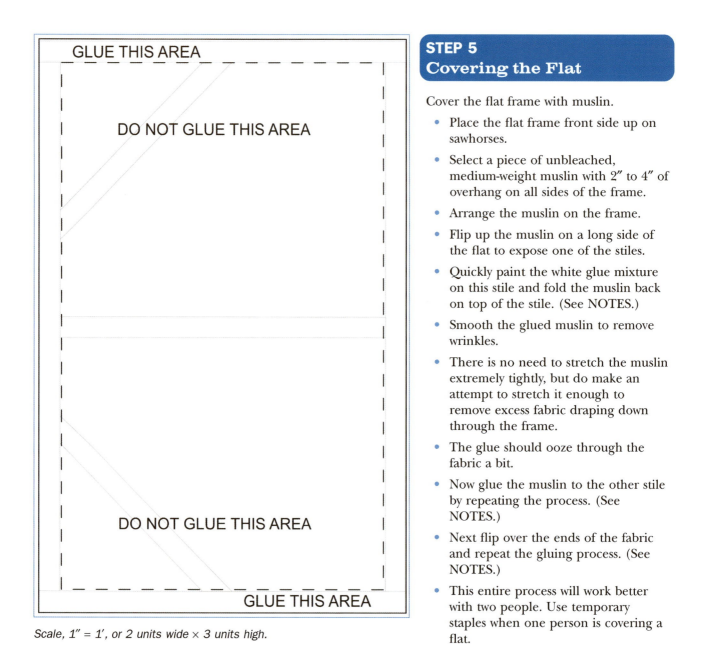

GLUE THIS AREA

DO NOT GLUE THIS AREA

DO NOT GLUE THIS AREA

GLUE THIS AREA

Scale, 1" = 1', or 2 units wide × 3 units high.

STEP 5
Covering the Flat

Cover the flat frame with muslin.

- Place the flat frame front side up on sawhorses.

- Select a piece of unbleached, medium-weight muslin with 2″ to 4″ of overhang on all sides of the frame.

- Arrange the muslin on the frame.

- Flip up the muslin on a long side of the flat to expose one of the stiles.

- Quickly paint the white glue mixture on this stile and fold the muslin back on top of the stile. (See NOTES.)

- Smooth the glued muslin to remove wrinkles.

- There is no need to stretch the muslin extremely tightly, but do make an attempt to stretch it enough to remove excess fabric draping down through the frame.

- The glue should ooze through the fabric a bit.

- Now glue the muslin to the other stile by repeating the process. (See NOTES.)

- Next flip over the ends of the fabric and repeat the gluing process. (See NOTES.)

- This entire process will work better with two people. Use temporary staples when one person is covering a flat.

NOTES

- Mix white glue at a ratio of 2 parts glue to 1 part water.

- There is no need to glue on top of the muslin. "Double gluing" was a popular technique when adhesives were of lesser quality. Excess glue will cause shiny spots and negatively affect the paint.

- The muslin will sag a bit when glued to the frame. This is expected. The muslin will shrink when sized.

- Large or unusually shaped flats might require staples to hold the muslin in place while drying; they should be removed after the muslin is dry.

STEP 6
Trimming and Surface Preparation

Prime the flat.

- The flat must be completely dry.

- Priming will shrink the muslin and remove the sag.

- Priming will prepare the surface for painting.

Possible priming materials:

- Laundry starch—A traditional and inexpensive primer that provides an excellent surface for painting.

- Wall size—A commercial product found in paint and hardware stores.

- Animal glue—Long used as a binder for dry pigment paints; also used as a primer.

- White glue—The same mixture used for gluing muslin to flat frames is also used as a primer (but with the addition of more water).

- Paint—Scenic paint with additional water will work as a primer but will not provide as nice a painting surface as the starch-based primers. (See NOTES.)

Scale, 1″ = 1′, or 2 units wide × 3 units high.

Applying the primer.

- Brush the primer and lightly work it on the muslin. *Do not scrub!*

- There is no need to force the primer through the fabric. If forced, the muslin will stick to the toggle and corner braces. (See NOTES.)

TRIMMING THE FLAT

- There are two philosophies for trimming the excess muslin:

  - Trim while the muslin is still wet. The muslin will not adhere to the very edge of the frame due to the drape of the fabric. Trimming the muslin at this time will fix this problem; however, trimming wet muslin is difficult.

  - Trim when the muslin is dry. Dry muslin is easier to trim, but there might be a little edge of the fabric that did not stick to the frame.

- Dry or wet, trim the muslin approximately 1/16″ to 1/8″ from the edge of the frame. Cut off a small bit of the corner. This will keep the muslin from pulling away from the flat frame during handling.

18

NOTES

- A small amount of paint in the primer will provide a toned or colored ground. The primer will be easier to see when priming the flat. The application will be more even.

- Applying a primer with a light touch is a good habit to start. Application technique is more important when larger pieces of scenery or full drops are primed. Excessive primer and force will add weight and stiffness to drops when painted vertically (Eastern style) and stick to floors when painted on the floor (Continental style). Research tips and techniques before working with scenery on a larger scale.

- It is possible that the edges of all the frame pieces will become apparent when a loaded brush is dragged over them. If this becomes a big problem, one solution is to use a hard-covered flat.

Things to Remember

STEP 7
Hard-Covered Flat

An alternative to a traditional flat is a hard-covered flat.

The hard covering can be:

- Plywood, usually 1/4″ thick
- Masonite®, either 1/8″ or 1/4″ thick (both of these are heavy for their size)
- Lauan, an inexpensive three-ply mahogany, usually 1/8″ thick

The frame can be constructed as a traditional flat frame with the addition of a hard covering.

The frame can also be constructed of 1 × 3′s with the wood placed on edge instead of on the flat. Construction techniques vary.

- The flat stays square because of the hard covering, so corner braces are eliminated.
- Plywood fasteners can still be used for extra strength.
- Metal angle irons can replace the plywood fasteners.

The many reasons to use a hard-covered flat might include:

- A wall section will take abuse.
- Wall wiggle is a problem because of door slams.
- Molding, trims, or pictures must be attached to the wall.

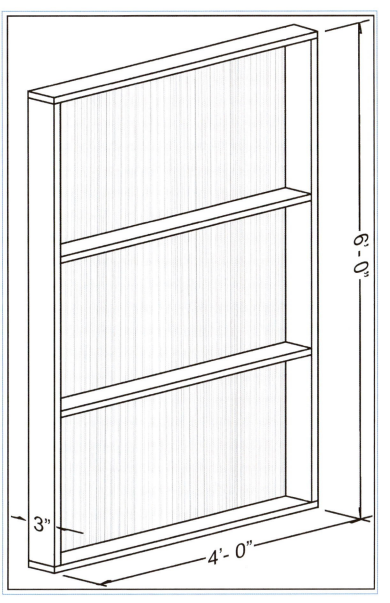

3"

4'- 0"

6'- 0"

Not to scale.

NOTES
- The grain of the hard covering will often appear even after the flat is primed. Seams between the hard coverings are difficult to hide. The hard covering might stain the paint, even after priming. If a quality surface is desired, the hard-covered flat can be covered (skinned) with muslin.
- The same white glue and water mixture is used to cover a hard flat. It is important not to stretch the muslin; instead, simply lay the muslin on the glued surface and pat it down. The wrinkles will disappear in a few minutes.

18

PROJECT 19
Final Project

WORK SURFACE

A 4′ × 6′ traditional or hard-covered flat.

TYPE OF PAINT

Rosco *Off Broadway* paint, Rosco *Iddings Deep Colors*, or a commercial latex substitute. See the COLOR SAMPLES page at the beginning of this book for brand and color suggestions.

TYPES OF CONSISTENCY

OUT OF THE CAN—Rosco suggests that the paint can be used right out of the can. This consistency might be thick. Add water to achieve a NORMAL consistency (see below).

NORMAL—Thick enough just to cover other projects in a single coat, assuming that the difference between the paint colors is not too great.

DILUTED—1 or 2 parts paint to 1 part water added to the NORMAL paint consistency.

WATERY—1 part paint to 5 to 10 parts water added to the NORMAL paint consistency. Rosco says: "Diluting with more than 2 parts water may reduce binder strength. Add Rosco *Clear Acrylic Glaze* to restore adhesion and flexibility."

PAINTING TECHNIQUES

This is a representative list. Every flat will include different techniques.

BASE PAINT (paint technique)—The first paint color or colors used in a specific painting project, usually the predominant color.

GRADED WET BLEND (paint technique)— Arranged in a scale or series; a smooth blend of gradated colors, usually in a linear pattern.

COMBING (paint technique)—A method of texturing using a brush with separated bristles to resemble the teeth of a comb (also called "dry brushing").

GRAINING (paint technique)—Creating a texture by dry brushing or combing to achieve the random patterns found in wood or marble.

MARBLING (paint technique)—Applying paint in a layer or layers to duplicate the look of marble.

SCUMBLE (paint technique)—A blend of two or more random patches of color; the size of the patches and the amount of blend will vary depending on the project.

SPATTER (paint technique)—A method of texture using a brush to throw drops of paint on a surface.

SPONGING (paint technique)—Creating a texture by applying paint with a sponge.

HIGHLIGHT WASH (paint technique)—A light, translucent paint used to represent the reflection of light or an area that receives the greatest amount of illumination.

SHADOW WASH (paint technique)—A dark, transparent paint used to suggest a shadow cast from one object on another.

Glossary

PAINT ELEVATION—A scaled, color drawing or painting of a piece of scenery provided by the scenic designer.

CARTOON—A line drawing of a paint elevation used as a guide for a painting project.

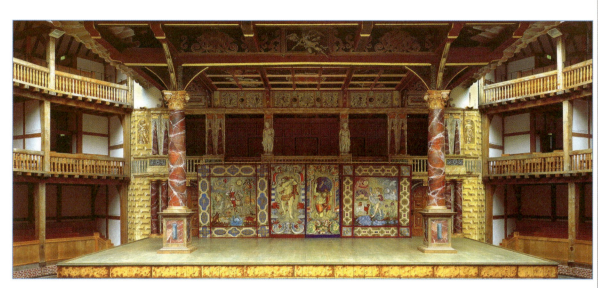

Scale, 1/4″ = 1′, or 7 units wide × 3 units high.

Light wood base Raw sienna - medium	**Light wall base** Cool gray - light		
Light wood #1 Raw sienna/burnt sienna	**Light wall #1** Sky blue - light		
Light wood #2 Burnt umber - medium	**Floor base** Chrome oxide green/ochre		
Dark wood base Burnt sienna	**Floor #1** Chrome oxide green - light		
Dark wood #1 Burnt umber	**Facing base** Lemon yellow		
Dark wood #2 Black	**Facing #1** Yellow ochre		
Tapestry #1 Deep red	**Tapestry #4** Pthalo blue		
Tapestry #2 Ultramarine blue	**Highlight wash** White/umber - 10% opacity		
Tapestry #3 Purple	**Shadow wash** Black/violet - 10% opacity		

TOOLS NEEDED
(See the Project pages for details.)

- **A collection of scene and housepainting brushes**

- **Chalk or charcoal for cartooning**

- **Tape measure and straightedge or lining stick**

- **Any additional equipment necessary to accomplish the desired results**

IMPORTANT!
- The color samples above represent the start of a set of paint colors. Additional colors might be needed, and not all colors are needed for every flat.

PAINT ELEVATION SEPARATED INTO INDIVIDUAL PROJECTS

Identify individual project flats by the number assigned in this key.

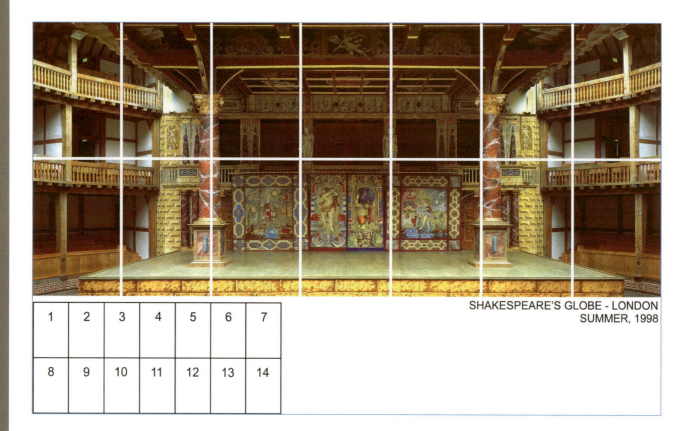

SHAKESPEARE'S GLOBE - LONDON
SUMMER, 1998

1	2	3	4	5	6	7
8	9	10	11	12	13	14

IMPORTANT!

- A final project might be desirable if this book is used in a situation that lends itself to a capstone experience. This is an example of a possible final assignment, but the possibilities for a project of this kind are endless. Be creative in your choice.

GOALS OF THE PROJECT

- Painters learn to work together and get along as a group.

- The painting experience mirrors real-world situations. Working and sharing as a group are to be expected when working on a production.

- This project should be complicated. Most painters want the challenge and a chance to showcase their cumulative skills.

- A complicated project skillfully executed is good for the painter's self esteem.

- A project of this type carefully presented is a great addition to a portfolio.

Flat #1; scale, 2 units wide × 3 units high.

Flat #2; scale, 2 units wide × 3 units high.

THE GLOBE AS A FINAL PROJECT

- This project is based on pictures taken of Shakespeare's Globe in London.

- It is a challenging project with a rather high degree of difficulty but also a high degree of potential success.

- Aspects of the actual façade are painted and interesting to reproduce.

- The project can be adjusted to different skill levels if painters are allowed to trade assignments or if they are assigned tasks according to their abilities by an instructor.

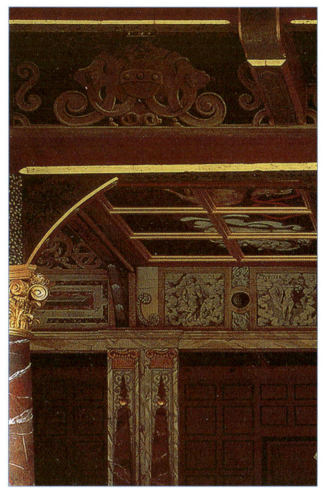

Flat #3; scale, 2 units wide × 3 units high.

Flat #4; scale, 2 units wide × 3 units high.

Final Project

TYPES OF POSSIBLE PROJECTS

- Projects painted in my classes have included a car from a parts catalog, an ad from a magazine, a complete book jacket, and paintings from art books.

- Choose between photographs or paintings. Pick a format best suited to the group.

- Painters respond well to challenging projects.

- The project presented here is based on an amateur photograph of Shakespeare's Globe. Other projects might be reproductions of copyrighted materials, which will limit the reproduction possibilities.

Final Project

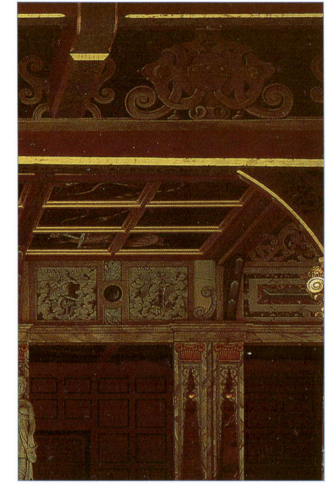

Flat #5; scale, 2 units wide × 3 units high.

Flat #6; scale, 2 units wide × 3 units high.

FINAL SIZE OF THE PROJECT

- If the number of painters is a prime number, someone will have to paint an extra flat (perhaps an instructor, guest, or previous painter).

- Remember that flats can be turned in either direction. Twelve 4′ × 6′ flats can form a final surface of 16′ × 18′ or 24′ × 12′ (or the reverse)

- Pick a source picture of a specific size and complexity that reflects the number of painters participating in the project.

- Photo-manipulation software is extremely helpful, perhaps mandatory, in preparing the project.

Flat #7; scale, 2 units wide × 3 units high.

Flat #8; scale, 2 units wide × 3 units high.

PROCEDURE FOR PROJECT DISTRIBUTION

- Slips of paper numbered to represent the total flats in the project are chosen at random by the painters.

- Decide if it is acceptable for painters to trade projects. If left on their own, painters could trade projects with others to make use of their strengths; however, there is the potential for hurt feelings.

- Handing out assignments based on painters' strengths is likely in a production environment.

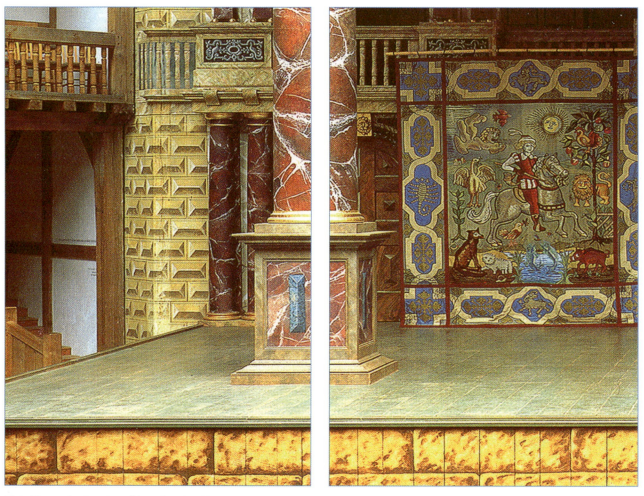

Flat #9; scale, 2 units wide × 3 units high.

Flat #10; scale, 2 units wide × 3 units high.

PROCEDURE FOR PAINTING

- All the painting could take place during supervised time, but it is more likely that painting will occur without supervision. What rules can be established and enforced without requiring the presence of an instructor?

- To what degree will instruction be used to inform painters about the process? Answering questions instead of lecturing is one approach.

- Left on their own, painters will tend to mix paint as a group. Is this acceptable? How would paint get mixed in a production setting?

- Lining up shared edges of neighboring flats will require organization and cooperation.

Flat #11; scale, 2 units wide × 3 units high.   *Flat #12; scale, 2 units wide × 3 units high.*

PROCEDURE FOR PAINTING

- Set standards for when and where the painting will take place.

- How much time should be allotted for painting the project? It is possible that, regardless of the allotted time, the majority of painting will be accomplished the night before the presentation.

- Consider intermediate deadlines if last-minute painting is not acceptable.

- The project should foster group responsibility and helpfulness.

- Consider photographing intermediate steps in the painting process.

Flat #13; scale, 2 units wide × 3 units high.   *Flat #14; scale, 2 units wide × 3 units high.*

PRESENTATION OF THE FINAL PROJECT

- A festive mood is typical during the presentation of an assignment (and food is usually involved in the celebration).

- Although the paint must be dry, the final cleanup is usually postponed to this time.

- Consider inviting guests to view the work. It is interesting for them to see the finished product and their good wishes help to validate the work.

- Will the finished product be on public display? Is it possible or desirable for the work to hang in a theatre space?

- What happens to the work in the future? Are the flat frames recycled for the next group of painters? Remember, few things in theatre are permanent.

THE FINISHED PAINTING

- The final project was assembled on the paint frame in the rear of the stage.

- The frame was raised approximately 4' above the floor.

- The painters stood in front and struck characteristic poses.

- The scale of groundling to stage is incorrect, but it is does make for an interesting photograph.

Shakespeare's Globe

Final painting project

Painted December 18, 2002

by THEA 445 Scene Painting

Department of Theatre and Dance

University of Wisconsin, Stevens Point

RESULT OF THE EXPERIENCE

- Painters tend to put in extra effort when a group outcome is at stake. They also help each other for the same reason.

- Painters are very proud of their work. This exercise gives them a chance to see their work as the center of attention. This seldom happens in a production setting.

- The finished product can add interest to a theatre space. The displayed project could help motivate the next group of painters.

- Take plenty of photographs!